The JEWELER'S CRAFT

THE JEWELER'S CRAFT

Mastering Traditional Techniques

Jaime Pelissier

VNR VAN NOSTRAND REINHOLD COMPANY
New York Cincinnati Toronto London Melbourne

Technical Drawings and Workshop Sketches
by Jaime Pelissier
Renderings by Laurence T. Huddon
Text Translated by Serena Pelissier

Copyright © 1981 by Van Nostrand Reinhold
Company
Library of Congress Catalog Card Number
80-39912
ISBN 0-442-24336-7

All rights reserved. No part of this work covered by
the copyright hereon may be reproduced or used
in any form or by any means—graphic, electronic,
or mechanical, including photocopying, recording,
taping, or information storage and retrieval
systems—without written permission of the
publisher.

Printed in the United States of America

Published by Van Nostrand Reinhold Company
135 West 50th Street
New York, NY 10020

Van Nostrand Reinhold Limited
1410 Birchmount Road
Scarborough, Ontario M1P 2E7, Canada

Van Nostrand Reinhold Australia Pty. Ltd.
17 Queen Street
Mitcham, Victoria 3132, Australia

Van Nostrand Reinhold Company Limited
Molly Millars Lane
Wokingham, Berkshire, England

16 15 14 13 12 11 10 9 8 7 6 5 4 3 2 1

Library of Congress Cataloging in Publication Data

Pelissier, Jaime, 1940-
    The jeweler's craft.
    Includes index.
    1. Jewelry making.   I. Title.
TS725.P4413   739.27   80-39912
ISBN 0-442-24336-7

CONTENTS

INTRODUCTION   6

TECHNICAL DRAWING   8

GOLDSMITHING EXERCISES   19

JEWELRY EXERCISES   60

USEFUL FINDINGS EXERCISES   94

WORKSHOP NOTES   97

BIBLIOGRAPHY   109

INDEX   110

INTRODUCTION

During the 1970s, I worked in Mexico as general coordinator of a regional center for research and assistance in technology and design and then as head of the center's jewelry department. The post enabled me to visit jewelry schools in many countries. In Denmark, at the Goldsmiths, Silversmiths and Engravers Guild School, I found programs for technical training independent of design training. This kind of training was needed in Mexico. I developed a program of my own, with short, intensive modular courses, incorporating some of the exercises used at the Danish school. It was a solely technical program, aimed at developing qualified craftspeople in traditional jewelry making. The majority of exercises were based on pieces made by local craftspeople and pieces seen in magazines related to the trade, and unrelated to any modern design concept. Setting up the program involved analyzing the constructive aspects of the pieces, establishing the various steps in their fabrication, and then translating them into clear and precise technical drawings. The students in the center worked with a qualified master who used the exercises in his lessons to emphasize the necessary operations and basic skills required in jewelry making: cutting, piercing, filing, soldering, and forming.

In transforming the course material into a well-organized, useful workshop practice book, I ran into several difficulties, among them that the original exercise directions were abbreviated and would be insufficient if the student were to work without a qualified teacher; that the needs of another culture would be very different from those in Mexico; that the craftspeople in this country are a much more heterogeneous group than those in Latin America; and that there are a number of people here who work in metals but who have had no direct experience in production workshops—namely, students of art and design schools—who could also benefit from a book of this type.

This has required a radical revision of the program. I have eliminated several rather tedious exercises, even though they lend themselves to good discipline, and have included new ones. The instructions originally directed to the teacher are now in clear and precise lay language, describing the construction process of each piece.

I do not discuss *how* to cut, file, or solder, as these are subjects thoroughly described in many good books on jewelry making. In this way I can devote more attention to the technical aspects of construction, which I hope will give the reader-student the freedom to be able to express himself without difficulty in the more creative aspects of jewelry, a freedom which comes from mastering techniques and understanding the possibilities of metal.

The book will be most beneficial to the craftsperson who spends eight hours a day at the bench and who needs to expand his or her knowledge in the field. Industry or production shops do not allow the craftsperson to leave the mechanical, repetitive operations which are, unfortunately, indispensable to production. It does not intend to cover all of the subjects in traditional jewelry making, which would be almost impossible. It gives a very solid base and sufficient skills to start you in the continuous learning process that is fundamental in this craft.

TECHNICAL DRAWING

ORTHOGRAPHIC PROJECTION

If the exact measurements, angles, and curves of a piece are to be reproduced, it is practically impossible to base the job on the three-dimensional effect of a photograph or rendering. To establish the exact measurements, and thus the steps required for construction, it is necessary to present different views of the object, which indicate in detail all its forms and parts. These views are drawn in different positions, arranged systematically at right angles to each other.

This type of drawing is called orthographic projection. It is based on a system of four quadrants. In the majority of the exercises in the book, only two views are needed for the completion of the piece: front and top views, or front and right side, or front and left side. In more complex pieces, three or four views will be shown: front, top, and one or both sides.

Some exercises also require sectional drawings, to show hidden details. The section is usually set up on the axis of the piece, with two arrows at each end to indicate the direction of the view. The nearest plane is imagined to be transparent or removed, so that the interior of the object is visible.

The drawings in this book will be projected in the third quadrant. To represent the idea of quadrants more clearly, imagine a transparent box with an object inside it. Draw lines on the walls of the box as the object is seen from the front, from the top, and from the right side. Then open the box, extending the top and side walls so that the three walls are in one plane. We now have three views of an orthographic projection in the third quadrant.

TECHNICAL DRAWING 9

Thus:
1. Object drawn on walls of transparent box.
2. Walls extended to present three drawings in one plane.
3. Orthographic drawing showing six views.
   a. Front view
   b. Top view
   c. Left side view
   d. Right side view
   e. Bottom view
   f. Rear view

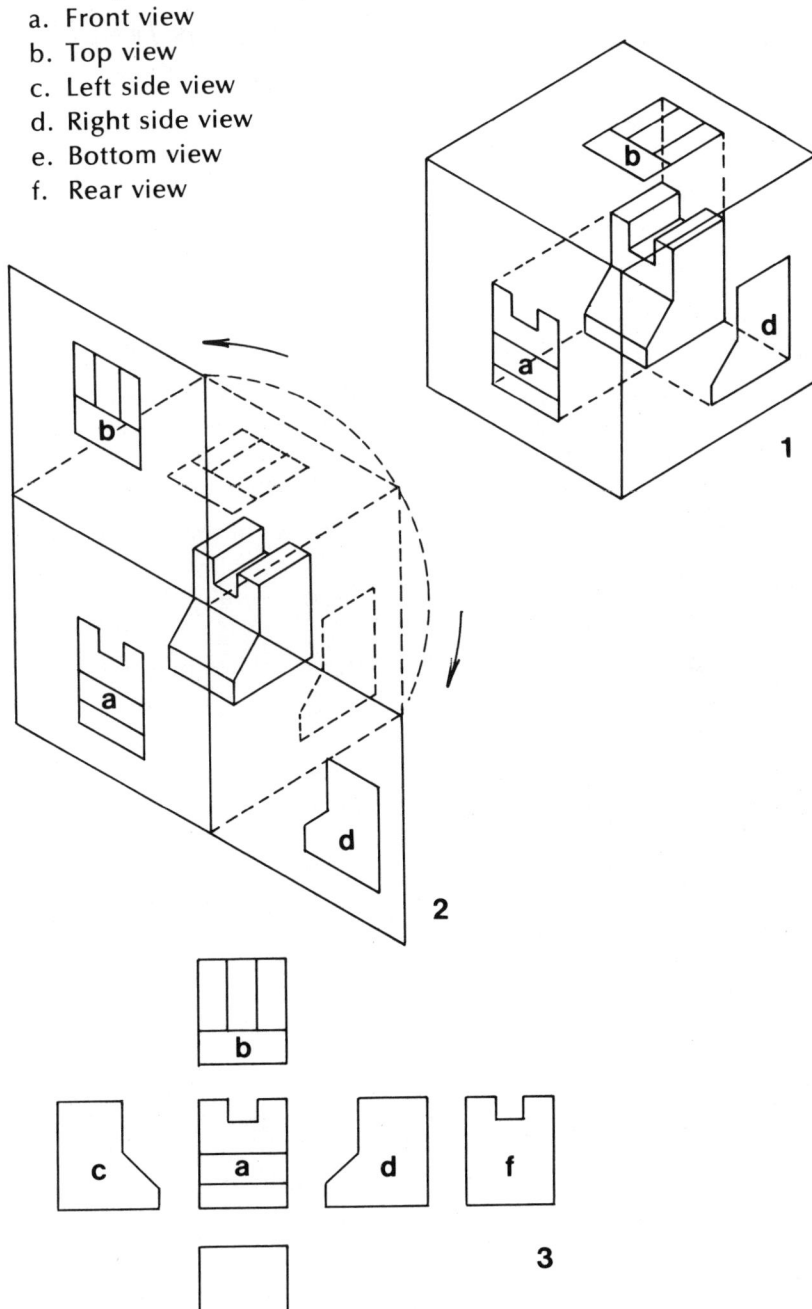

SCALE

In drawing small objects, the scale is usually enlarged so that details are readily seen. The scale of a drawing is expressed as the relation between the size of the object in the drawing and the real size of the object. Depending on the size of the object, scales such as 2:1, 3:1, and 5:1 are established, indicating that the object has been enlarged two, three, or five times, respectively. When the object is drawn in its actual size, the drawing is said to be in natural scale, or drawn to a scale of 1:1.

The scale is specified in each exercise. I have used only two scales: 1:1 and, for certain details only, 2:1. In some exercises all the details are drawn to a 2:1 scale; in these cases there is a sketch of the piece in 1:1 scale without details.

COMPARISON OF MEASUREMENTS

All the measurements given in the exercises are in millimeters, as the metric system is now nearly universal. To facilitate conversion from millimeters to thousandths of inches and American Standard gauge, I have included a table of equivalencies. The metric measurements given in the exercises may not coincide exactly with the equivalents in the table, and it will be necessary to find the nearest number in American Standard gauge or in thousandths of an inch, or to calculate it according to the conversion methods shown below.

In measuring lengths, we have:
1 inch (in.) = 25.4 millimeters (mm)
12 inches = 1 foot (ft.) = 30.48 centimeters (cm)

1 mm = 0.04 in. (approx. 1/25 in.)
10 mm = 1 cm = 0.4 in.
100 mm = 10 cm = 1 decimeter (dm) = 3.94 in.
1000 mm = 100 cm = 1 meter (m) = 39.37 in. = 3.28 ft. = 1.09 yard

To convert inches to millimeters, multiply by 25.4.
To convert millimeters to inches, multiply by 0.3937.

Comparison of Measurements

Inch	Millimeter	American Standard Gauge	Drill No.
.0142	0.361	27	79/80
.0159	0.404	26	78/79
.0179	0.455	25	77/78
.0201	0.511	24	75/76
.0226	0.574	23	73/74
.0253	0.643	22	71/72
.0285	0.724	21	69/70
.0320	0.813	20	67
.0359	0.912	19	64/65
.0403	1.024	18	59/60
.0453	1.151	17	56/57
.0508	1.290	16	55/56
.0571	1.450	15	53/54
.0641	1.629	14	51/52
.0720	1.829	13	49/50
.0808	2.052	12	46/47
.0907	2.304	11	42/43
.1019	2.588	10	37/38
.1144	2.906	9	32/33
.1285	3.264	8	30
.1443	3.670	7	26/27
.1620	4.111	6	19/20
.1819	4.618	5	14/15

BASIC CONCEPTS IN GEOMETRY

Throughout all the exercises, a good grasp of certain elementary concepts in geometry will be most useful. Only the most indispensable ones are included. If more information is needed, any textbook of plane geometry will serve as a reference. The elements given here are sufficient to achieve the layout of all the exercises.

To draw a right angle (an angle of 90°), mark point O on a straight line segment. Resting the compass point on this focus, draw arc AB. Resting the compass point first at A, then at B, draw two arcs that intersect at C. Draw a straight line between C and O. This line is perpendicular to AB and thus forms an angle of 90°.

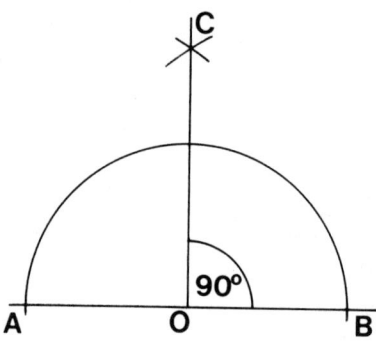

To bisect a straight line is to divide it into two equal parts. With the compass point on each end of a straight line segment AB, draw two arcs of equal radius longer than half of AB, so that they intersect above and below the line (points C and D). Join C and D with a straight line. This line divides the first line in half and is perpendicular to it.

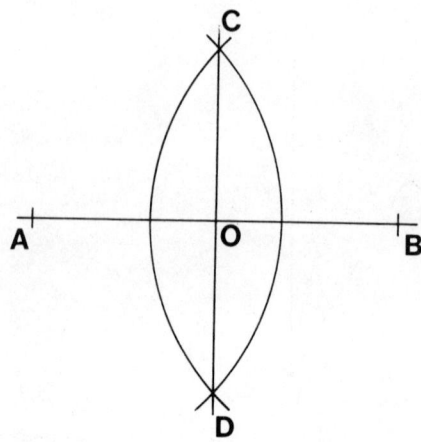

TECHNICAL DRAWING 13

To bisect an angle (the given angle here is AOB), draw an arc with a radius shorter than OA or OB, with its center at O, making points C and D. With the same radius, draw two arcs with centers at C and D, which intersect at E. OE will bisect angle AOB. This operation is the same for any angle.

To draw a 45° angle on a given straight line (AB), make an arc slightly longer than a quarter of a circle with a center at B and a radius of AB. Raise a line perpendicular to AB at B, extending it to intersect the arc at C. AC forms a 45° angle with AB.

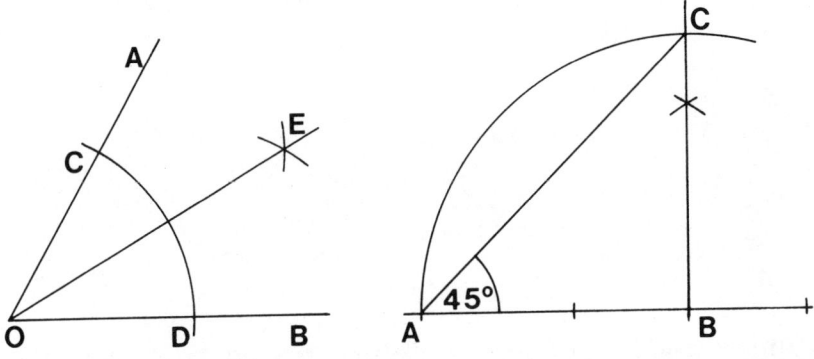

Some exercises require drawing multiple angles. On a given straight line, draw an arc with a center at A and a radius AB. With the same radius and center at B, cut the original arc, making point C. Angle CAB is 60°. To obtain a 120° angle, again use radius AB. With the center at C, cut the original arc at D. DAB is a 120° angle. Bisect CAB to obtain an angle of 30° (EAB). Bisect DAC to obtain an angle of 90° (FAB).

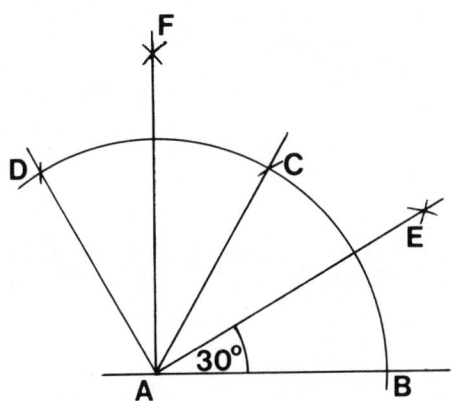

14 THE JEWELER'S CRAFT

To draw an equilateral triangle—a triangle with sides of equal length—mark two points A and B on a line segment. With the compass point at A and a radius of AB, draw an arc. Then, with the compass point at B and with the same radius, draw an arc that intersects the first at C. From point C draw two straight lines to A and B.

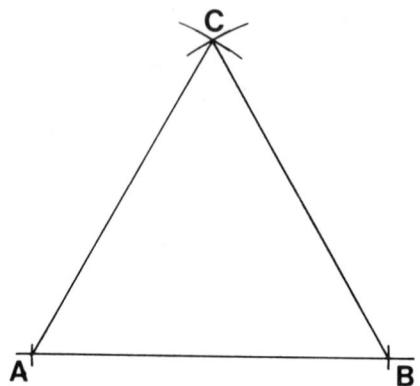

It is important to know the relation between the diameter of a circle and its circumference, its length around. This relationship is one of the most commonly used in jewelry making. Every time you need to know the length of a piece of metal to make rings, bezels, various settings, and spheres, this relationship is applied.

The circumference of a circle is obtained by multiplying the diameter by pi (π), approximately 3.1416. Thus a circle with a diameter of 20 mm has a circumference of
$$20 \text{ mm} \times 3.1416 = 62.832 \text{ mm}$$

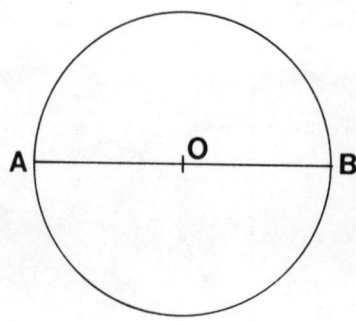

One method to draw an ellipse is the four-center method. Depending on the type of ellipse—the relation between its axes—other methods may be necessary. The exercise which involves drawing and cutting an ellipse uses the four-center method. This method is used when the shorter axis is at least two-thirds the length of the longer axis.

At the center O of a line segment AB (the ellipse's longer axis), draw a perpendicular CD, which will become the ellipse's shorter axis. With the center at O and a radius equal to the length of AB minus the length of CD, mark points E and F. With the center at O and a radius the length of three-quarters of line OF, mark points G and H. Draw straight lines that join EH, EG, FH, and FG and extend them beyond the projected perimeter of the ellipse.

With the center at E and radius ED, draw arc KDL; with the center at F and radius FC, draw arc ICJ opposite it. With the center at H and radius HB, draw arc JBL that joins two ends of these arcs. Finally, with the center at G and radius GA, draw arc IAK which joins this side to the two original arcs.

The circumference of the ellipse equals one-half the length of the longer axis plus one-half the length of the shorter axis multiplied by π (3.1416). Thus, an ellipse with a longer axis of 20 mm and a shorter axis of 16 mm has a circumference of

$$(10 \text{ mm} + 8 \text{ mm}) \times 3.1416 = 50.2656 \text{ mm}$$

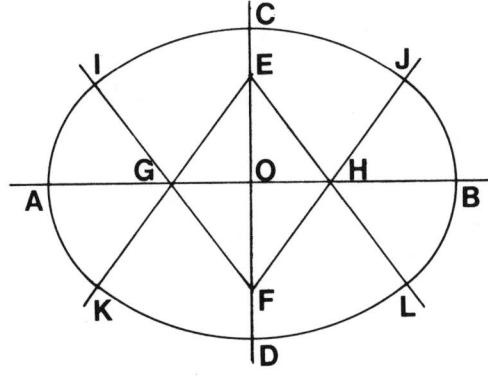

To draw a hexagon, draw a circle with diameter AB. With the same radius (OB) and A and B as centers, describe two arcs which intersect the circumference. Join the six foci with straight lines.

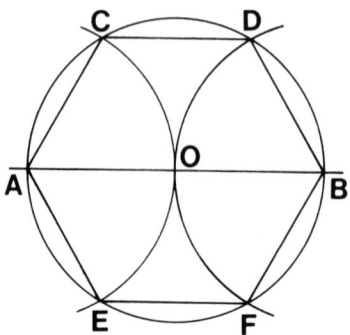

To draw a pentagon, draw a circle with diameter AB, and a radius OC perpendicular to AB. Bisect OB. With point D as center and radius DC, draw arc CE. With center C and radius CE, draw arc EF. CF is a side of the pentagon. With this opening in the compass, cut the circle in five equal segments and join the foci.

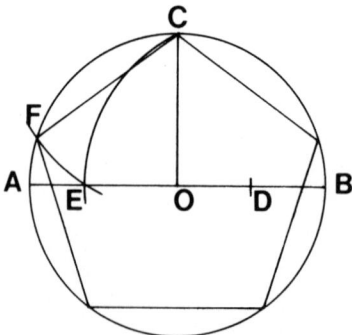

You will often need to establish a center in a geometric figure. When using regular or symmetrical figures with an equal number of sides, you can use diagonals to find the geometric center, which is the point where the diagonals intersect. The diagonals can also be used to simplify the construction of a figure. In (a), intersecting diagonals indicate the geometric center; in (b), they are used to draw inscribed or circumscribed figures; in (c), they are used to enlarge or reduce figures of the same base; in (d), they enlarge or reduce a geometric form.

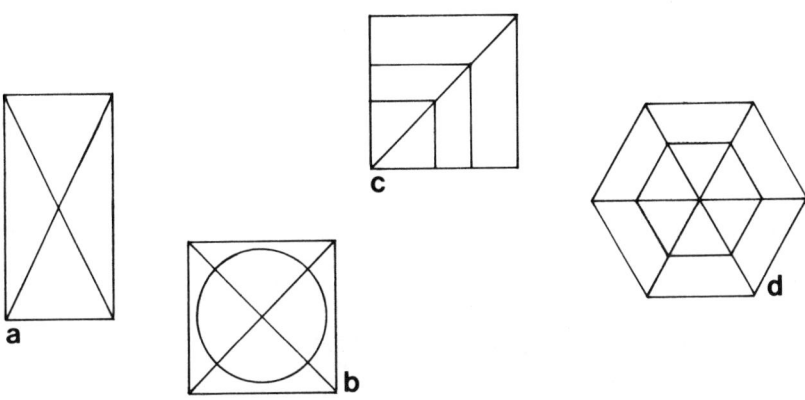

A straight line can be divided into a number of equal parts. Straight line AB is to be divided into seven equal parts. Draw a perpendicular AC at A. Place a ruler on a slanted line between B and the perpendicular so that seven equal parts are included. Mark these points and draw perpendicular lines between them and AB, thus dividing AB into seven equal parts.

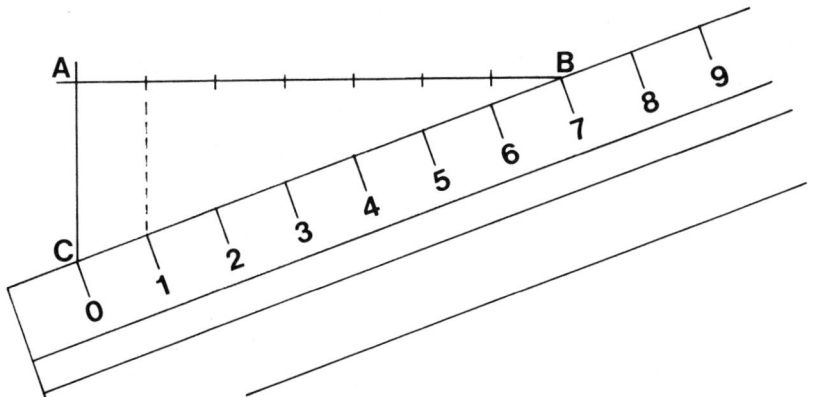

To divide a circle into equal parts, on a straight line, draw a circle with its center at O and diameter AB. Divide the diameter into the same number of equal parts as the circle is to be divided into. This can be done either by using a ruler or by using the method above for dividing a straight line into equal parts. The precision of this marking will determine the precision of the final division of the circle.

With the compass point at A and the pencil at B, and then with the point at B and the pencil at A, draw arcs that cross at C. From C, draw a straight line that passes through D, the second division of the diameter, and that will cross the perimeter at E. EB is the distance required to divide the perimeter into the desired number of parts. Open the compass to the length of EB and mark the divisions on the perimeter. If the distance is not marked precisely, the last division will not meet point E perfectly.

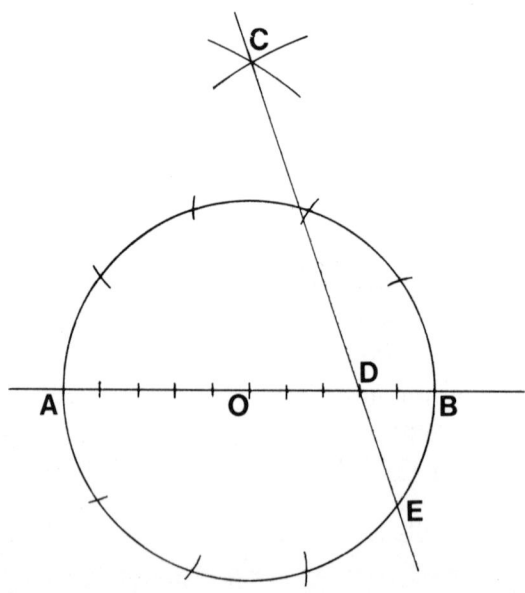

GOLDSMITHING EXERCISES

Traditionally, in Europe especially, a distinction is made between specific jewelry skills. Some schools even teach the specialties as separate courses. These distinct fields are goldsmithing and jewelry.

A goldsmith, in the traditional sense, works in precious metals making personal ornaments and objects that do not necessarily include precious stones. A jeweler makes personal ornaments in which precious stones are fundamental. The two specialties are obviously connected, as both require knowledge of precious metals and use the same techniques. Usually specialists in each branch are fully capable of working in the other.

I have made a division here between goldsmithing and jewelry techniques, following this traditional distinction and also to help in the progressive development of the exercises. The formation of traditional jewelry skills is based on techniques described in this chapter.

These exercises begin with the most basic elements and progress to fairly complicated exercises. The exercises for jewelers should not be begun until the goldsmithing exercises have been mastered. The only stones involved here are cabochon cut, and the technique for making their setting is considered part of the goldsmithing field.

EXERCISES 1 THROUGH 6
   Objective: Sawing
   Materials: Brass, 1 mm thick; saw blades, 0 or 2/0
   Scale: 1:1

Exercises 1 through 6 are designed to give the necessary training for mastering one of the most important steps in jewelry making: sawing. A great deal of the final result of a piece depends on the quality of the cut. The exercises also offer practice in using the compass, a very useful instrument for layout.

Once mastered, sawing should be done as close to the indicated line as possible, leaving the line as the outside edge of the final piece. However, in these exercises, as practice and as an aid for fine execution, the sawing should be done right on the line itself, without going off it. Besides the difficulty of following the line exactly, the exercises present the problem of curves and angles of varying degrees. Once the straight line has been mastered, the curve is undertaken, as in the final exercises in this series. A helpful tip for turning angles: place the saw in a vertical position, do not put any forward pressure on it and accelerate the rhythm of the movement while simultaneously turning the frame of the saw on its axis. With a little practice, the angle will be done perfectly.

EXERCISE 1:   Square

Layout: The basic element in tracing a square is the right angle. A right angle can be easily made with a steel square. If one is not available, a right angle can be made with a compass, as described in Technical Drawing, Basic Concepts in Geometry.

Once the right angle is drawn, the length of its sides is determined with the compass, according to the measurement of the side of the square to be executed. The operation can be repeated, raising another right angle on a third side, or you can use a ruler to measure equal lengths parallel to those already drawn and thus form the other two sides.

This exercise gives practice in turning the saw to form right angle cuts and, finally, an acute angle cut. When the square is drawn, begin sawing *outside* the line. Then file up to the line the four sides. To trace the lines of the inside of the square, open the compass to the distance between the edge of the square and the first line.

Resting the metal on the bench, draw the lines so that the compass is supported on the edge of the metal and runs the length of it. This way the inside lines will be drawn exactly. The first compass opening draws the first four lines and is then widened to draw the two interior lines. Draw the diagonal last.

To help see the lines on the metal, I suggest painting the sheet with layout fluid, such as steel blue, or with some other coloring.

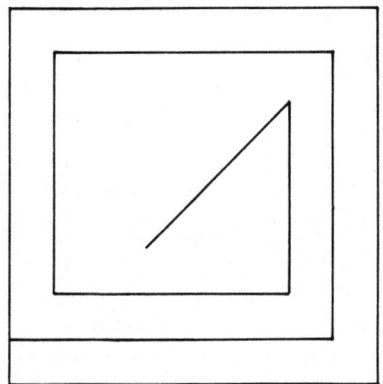

EXERCISE 2: **Rhomboid**

Layout: The manner of drawing is similar to that in Exercise 1. The only difference is in the outside line, which can be drawn with a protractor or, in this case, a 30–60 steel square. The exterior angle in this exercise is 60°. Inside lines are drawn as in Exercise 1. The exercise alternates acute angle cuts with obtuse angle cuts.

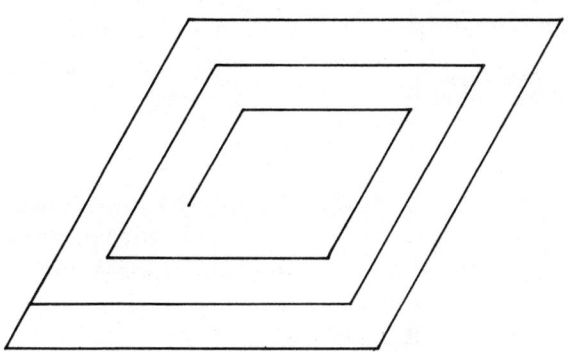

EXERCISE 3: Triangle

Layout: Use a compass to draw the triangle, although you could also use a protractor. This is an equilateral triangle; see the section on Basic Concepts in Geometry for drawing a triangle. The inside lines follow the method described in Exercise 1.

EXERCISE 4: Pentagon

Layout: Drawing a pentagon is extremely useful in many operations of jewelry making, particularly because it divides a circle into five equal parts. The section on Basic Concepts in Geometry describes the drawing process. Remember that once drawn, it must be cut and filed to the line; then the inside lines are drawn. The lines connecting each pentagon with the one inside it are drawn from the centers of one of the angles to the center of the pentagon.

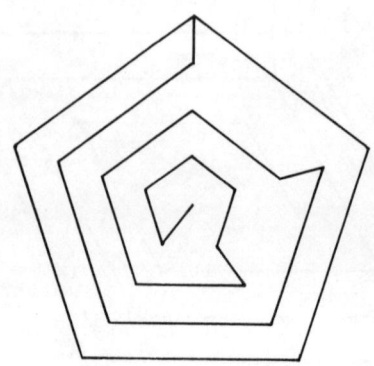

GOLDSMITHING EXERCISES 23

EXERCISE 5: **Circle**

Layout: This is one of the simplest shapes to draw. You may draw either the inner or the outer circle first, according to the measurements given. Open or close the compass the distance between the concentric circles to draw the following ones. (In this exercise, the inside lines are *not* drawn by resting the compass on the outside edge.) The whole exercise can be drawn before the outer circle is cut. The lines which connect one circle to another are closer together at the center because the circles decrease in size. All lines are directed from the circumference toward the center.

EXERCISE 6: **Ellipse**

Layout: The ellipse is a commonly used shape in jewelry making, but it is not always easy to draw. Templates such as those used in technical drawings are often used, and these are recommended in most cases. But it is sometimes important to know how to draw an ellipse, and this is the reason for this exercise. Here we have an ellipse with four centers; this technique is described in the section on Basic Concepts in Geometry. The rest of the drawing uses the system described in Exercise 1, resting the compass on the outside edge of the figure.

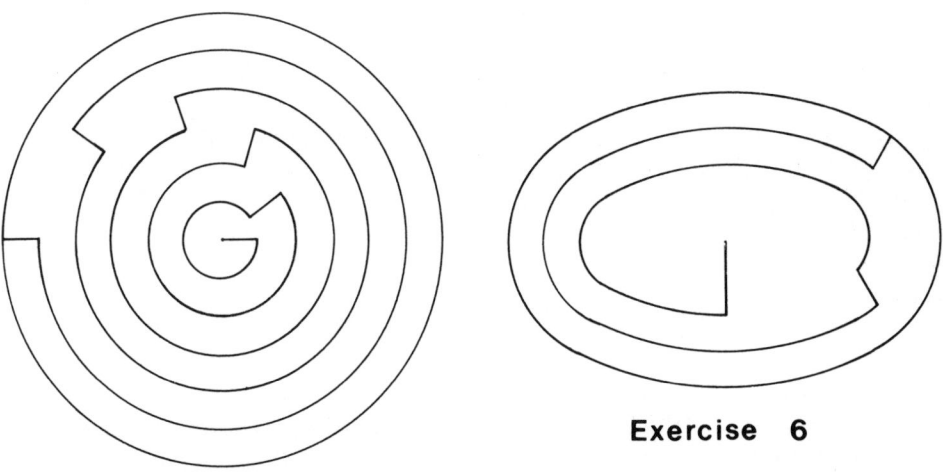

Exercise 5

Exercise 6

EXERCISES 7 AND 8

Objective: Sawing and drilling
Materials: Brass, 1 mm thick; saw blades, 0 or 2/0
Scale: 1:1

These exercises are designed to teach the use of drill bits and to give practice in drilling, as well as sawing between two or more perforations. Control of the drill on the metal is important for piercing and in work with stones with pavé settings, where the stones must be set with equal distances between them

EXERCISE 7: Angle Sawing between Two Drilled Points

Although this exercise has some perforations, which must be connected, it is actually more related to the preceding exercises. The main objective is, having made the drawing, to cut according to the drawing, remembering that the turning angles are *not* sharp but slightly rounded. Follow a straight line with the saw, arrive at the corner and turn with the smallest curve possible without making a right angle, and enter the other straight line immediately. It is probable that the frame of a normal saw will not reach the whole cut if it is begun from just one side, so I recommend starting from the other side once the center or the limit of the saw frame is reached, and joining the first line cut.

Layout: First draw the rectangle, cut it and file it. Define the distance between the lines (5 mm) and, using a steel square resting on the long side of the rectangle, draw all the parallel lines in the figure. Projecting a line from the upper drilled point of the rectangle to its opposite corners will give us the intermittent sides of the figure.

EXERCISE 8: Drilling on Intersecting Lines

Layout: Once the square is drawn (50 mm x 50 mm), draw lines parallel to its sides with a distance between them of 5 mm. All the intersecting points of the lines should be lightly marked with a center punch. After cutting the square and filing its sides, make all the perforations on the indicated points. The drill bit used should not be more than 1 mm in diameter. Connect some of the perforations with a saw, as shown.

GOLDSMITHING EXERCISES 25

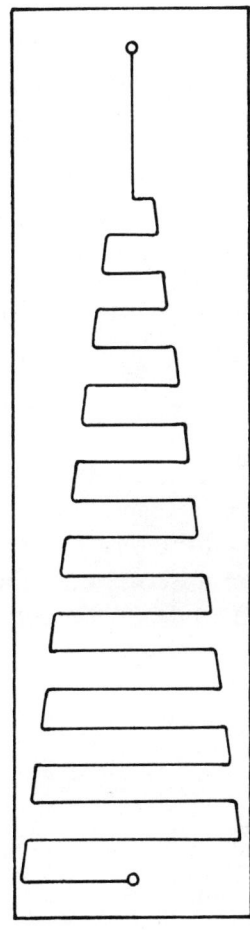

Exercise 7

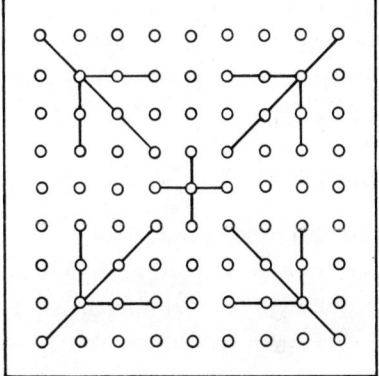

Exercise 8

EXERCISES 9 AND 10

Objective: Piercing
Materials: Brass, 1 mm thick; saw blades, 0 or 2/0
Scale: 1:1

Piercing is used a great deal in traditional jewelry making. These exercises should give a basis, beginning with cutting on a flat surface. Control of piercing, and therefore of the saw, is immensely important in opening lights in certain types of pavé settings and other operations. Beginning with these exercises, the metal should be cut as close to the drawn line as possible, without touching it. This allows for control in the later filing, which should leave the drawn line right on the edge without going beyond it. In cutting the circle, the cut should be made outside the line; when cutting inside the details, the cut should be inside the line, leaving the line itself in the final piece.

EXERCISE 9:   Layout and Piercing a Rosette

Layout and cut of the rosette: First draw the inside, smallest circle. Next draw the exterior circle with the greatest diameter. Then draw the third circle near the outside one (2.5 mm distance) which will define the limit of the piercing. Holding the opening of the compass absolutely steady, rest one arm of the compass on any point of the

inner circle circumference and draw an arc which cuts this circumference in two points. Place the point of the compass on either of these two points and repeat drawing the arcs until all the arms of the central rosette are drawn. If the angle of the compass is altered the slightest bit, the points will not meet precisely. Resting the compass on one of the points of the central rosette, open it 4 mm more, until you meet the little curve of the trianglelike form between the leaves of the rosette. Draw all of these, changing the resting point of the compass to each of the points of the rosette. When these are drawn, use a fine bit to perforate all the parts to be pierced—the leaves of the rosette and the triangular forms between them. Do not perforate the center, which is to be left solid.

EXERCISE 10: **Layout and Piercing (another) Rosette**

Layout and cut of the rosette: This exercise is slightly more complicated than the previous one. Divide the circle into eight parts; first divide it in four, drawing perpendicular lines through the center.

As it is very important to be able to analyze pieces and drawings in order to copy them, I will here ask the student to analyze the rosette, basing the analysis on the experience learned in the previous exercises, to decide his own layout with no further indications. The parts to be pierced are the triangularlike figures, the comma-shaped figures, and the center.

EXERCISES 11 THROUGH 14

Objective: Construction of simple forms; use of solder; emphasis on precision
Materials: Brass, 0.8 mm thick, unless another thickness is specified; saw blades, 2/0
Scale: 1:1

The execution of simple geometric forms requires great precision, as the parts must fit and the symmetry will reveal any defect in fabrication.

EXERCISE 11: Constructing a Square-Base Pyramid

Layout: Draw a square on the metal (dotted lines, fig. a). Using a compass, draw the respective triangles on each side of the square, as shown in the figure.

Construction: Saw the outside edges of the pyramid as drawn on the plane and file, being careful not to deform the triangles (a). Using an engraver, make a deep cut along the lines of the four sides of the square. With the line well defined, begin to file, using a triangle needle file (#1 or #2), along the sides of the square and bases of the triangles to produce a V cut (b). The angles of this cut should allow the four triangles, when raised, to meet in the top point of the pyramid. The turning movement for each triangle will be more than 90°, so the angle of the cut must be greater than 90°. It is also important that the cut be deep enough so that, when bending the triangles up, the metal is not displaced, rising above the base square and leaving a gap that would be impossible to fill.

Once the angles of the base are cut, file the edges of the sides of each triangle in a similar manner (b). With the sides filed, bend the four triangles very carefully (the metal must be annealed before you do this) so that all four meet in one point. Tie them and solder. Use enough solder to solder the bases of the triangles as well as the sides (c).

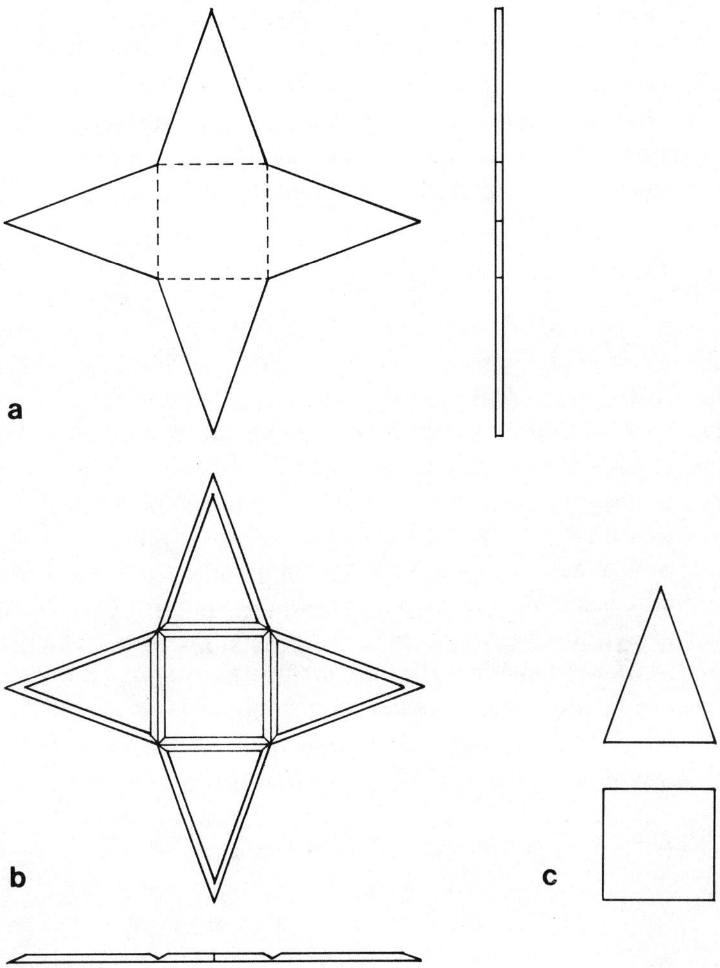

GOLDSMITHING EXERCISES 29

a

b

c

EXERCISE 12: **Constructing a Frame with the Bases of Four Interior Triangles Soldered on the Interior Sides of the Frame**

Material: Square wire for frame, 2 mm per side

The length of the wire for the frame is found by multiplying the length of a side of the square by four. Once this dimension is established, cut the wire (a) and proceed to make V cuts with a 90° opening at the points which will be the corners of the square. Make 45° cuts on each end (b). Anneal the metal and then bend it to form the square (c), and solder the four corners immediately. It is important before soldering to make sure the four angles are perfect right (90°) angles. If the cut has not been made with perfect precision, it will be practically impossible to form exact right angles. One of the most common errors is a slight displacement of one of the cuts, resulting in a totally irregular figure, with one side longer than the other and angles of various degrees.

Proceed to cut the four interior triangles (d), making sure they are all exactly alike, and solder them on the inside edge of the frame. Be sure the distance between each face of the triangles and the edges of the frame are exactly the same (e). The best method for soldering them is to place the frame on an absolutely flat surface of new charcoal or asbestos (the former is recommended because of the hazards of asbestos), and place a square piece of metal of the necessary height inside the frame, making sure it does not touch the frame at any point. Place the triangles to be soldered on this piece of metal; the figure should resemble (f) when completed, with a tiny line of separation between the triangles.

EXERCISE 13: **Constructing a Cube**

The procedure is very similar to that of the preceding exercise. First determine the length of the strip which will form the four sides of the cube by adding the lengths of each side. Make the same V cuts described in Exercise 12, with the same angles (a). Bend the four sides and solder the corners. If the sides of this open cube are perfectly square, file them until they are slightly rectangular (b), remembering that their respective covers will be soldered onto the open parts, compensating for the change in measurement and making them square. Cut the two covers slightly larger than the sides of the cube (c) and solder first one, then the other (d). Finally, file off the excess metal so that the sides are as shown in (e).

GOLDSMITHING EXERCISES 31

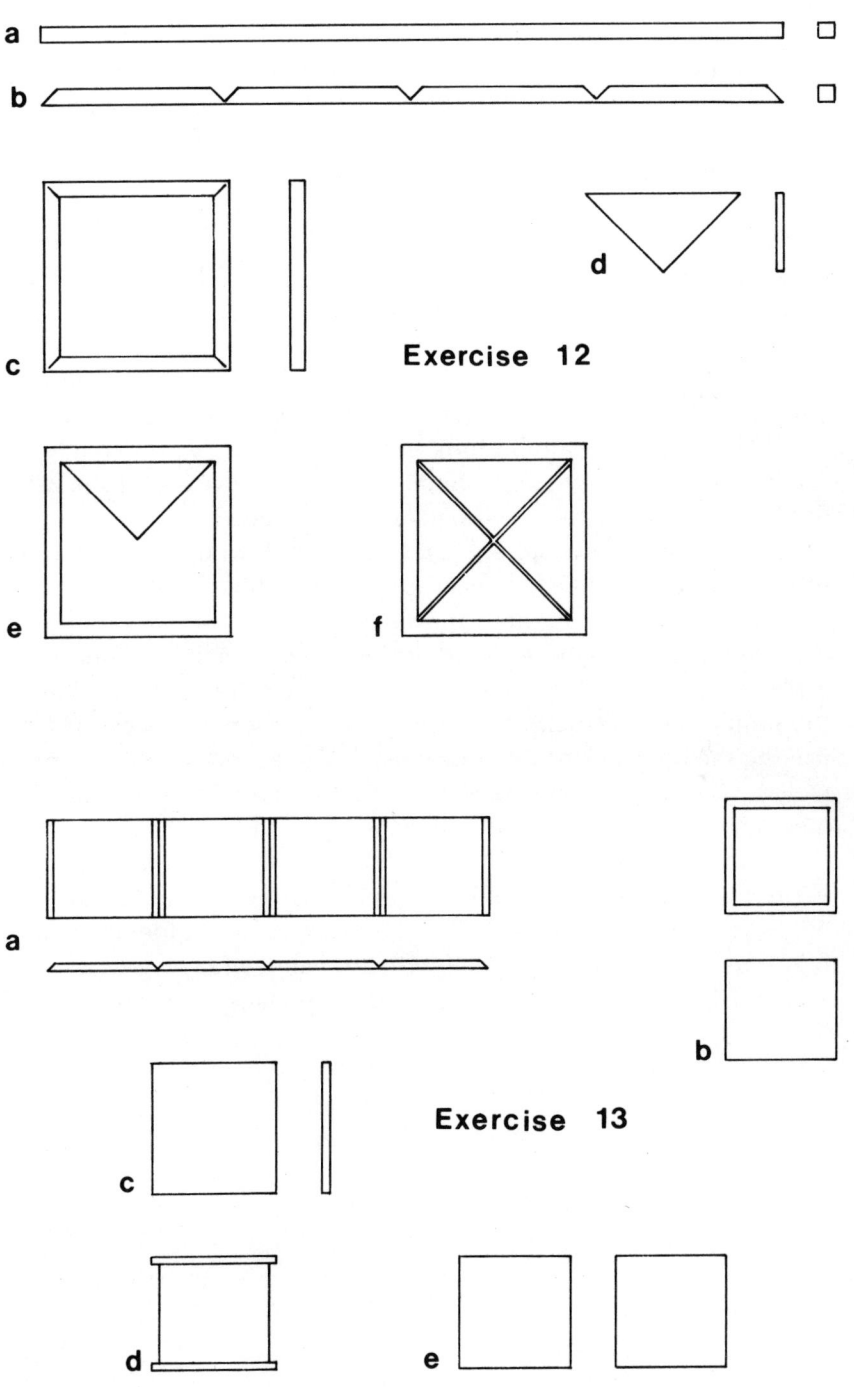

Exercise 12

Exercise 13

EXERCISE 14: Constructing a Sphere

Cut two discs with the diameter indicated in (a), and file the edges. In the process of embossing the disc to form a hemisphere, its diameter diminishes between 20 and 25 percent, depending on the thickness of the metal and the form of embossing. Begin by placing the disc on the larger hollow of a dapping block (the disc should just fit inside the circumference of the hollow) and emboss the metal, using dapping punches as close as possible to the diameter of the hollow. Allow for the thickness of the metal to achieve the most even form possible and not expand the metal excessively in the center. At the same time, this allows the metal to enter into the hollow without damaging the edges when touching the hollow's edges. Anneal the metal at least once during the embossing process. The two discs should look like those in (b), with diameters exactly twice the height of the hemisphere. Otherwise the form will not be perfect when the two parts are soldered.

The two parts of the sphere can be held with wrapping wire and soldered directly, but when making spheres of this size or smaller, I recommend putting an interior ring along the joining line to hold the two faces perfectly centered during the moment of soldering.

Measure the interior diameter of one of the spheres and multiply this number by 3.1416 (π). The result will be the length necessary for making the interior ring, as shown in (c). Cut a piece of metal 2 mm wide by the length just established and file the edges. Anneal the metal, bending it so you can solder the two ends, and shape it on a ring mandrel. The finished ring is shown in (d).

Then solder the ring on one of the hemispheres (e). Adjust the edges so the second half fits, eliminating any excess solder from the first union. Tie the second half with annealed wrapping wire and solder. File the excess solder and sand the surface of the sphere, as in (f).

GOLDSMITHING EXERCISES 33

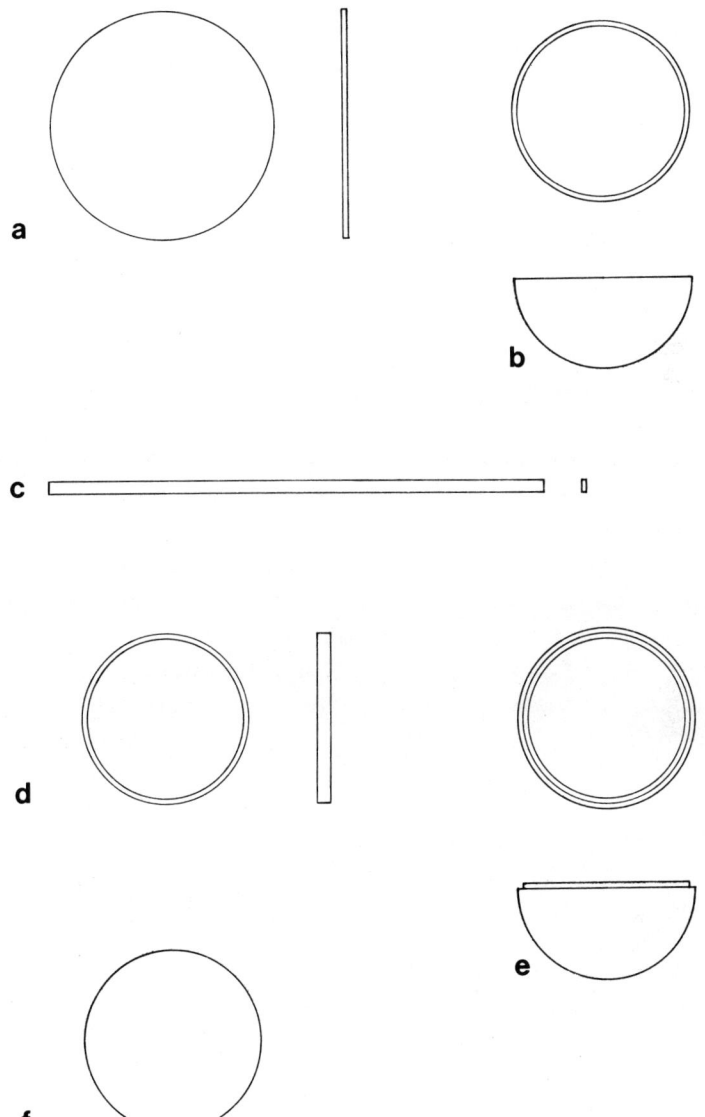

EXERCISES 15 THROUGH 22

Objective: Filing
Materials: Brass, rod of 4 mm square section or any equivalent (a bar of ϕ (diameter) 6 mm can be reduced and drawn to the necessary measurement, 4 mm x 2.75 mm); files, 8-in. flat file cut #1 or #2 for lateral surfaces of rings, 6-in. half-round for upper parts and details, assortment of needle files
Scale: 1:1

Although these exercises begin with ring bands, the emphasis is on teaching how to file reduced and difficult surfaces, where any error in the work is very evident. Beginners tend to use very small files, and therefore the proper file for each exercise will be indicated.

As this series of exercises deals with eight rings, it is recommended to make all eight at the same time before going on to the individual filing operations. The sizes of the rings should be different; for example, two or three #5, two or three #6, etc.

The way to calculate the necessary length for the wire or piece of metal to make the band is to multiply the interior diameter of the ring by 3.1416 (π) and add the thickness of the metal multiplied by two. In the case of these exercises, the figure shows an unspecified length (a). After annealing the metal, bend it in a curve to form a ring which remains open at the meeting of the two ends (b). Note that a V-shaped section is left open in the ring, which is why two times the thickness of the metal is added to arrive at the correct diameter of the finished ring. The interior of the ring is, at this point, larger than necessary. Cut the points of contact with a saw (c). Close the ring and solder.

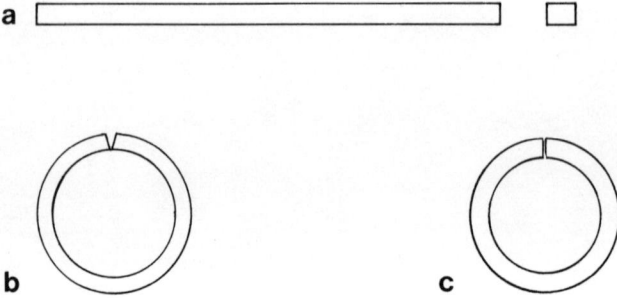

When the ring is soldered it is not yet round. Place the ring around a mandrel and hammer it while pushing it up the mandrel until you form a perfectly round ring.

When all the rings are ready, file the edges so that the two are perfectly parallel. First file one; then, opening a compass to the proper width, trace a line around the outside surface of the ring, resting one side on the filed edge, and being sure the line drawn is perfectly parallel to it. The second edge is then filed to the line.

EXERCISE 15: Flat Finger Band

In this exercise you will file the outside (upper) surface of the rings, continuing the basic operation for all the following ring exercises.

The upper surface is flat. With a compass resting on the inside of the ring, draw a line on the edge parallel to the inside curve. Repeat this on the other side of the ring. This will determine the distance between the inside of the ring and the outside edge, and is a necessary step because the ring may have become somewhat deformed while being hammered on the mandrel. File the outside surface to the lines drawn on the edge, thereby making the exterior and interior surfaces perfectly parallel.

EXERCISE 16: Channeled Finger Band

Make a channel 1 mm deep and 2 mm thick, along the circumference of the ring; this leaves two edges of 1 mm each.

Draw the outside lines of the channel using a compass. Before using the file, you can use a fine saw, cutting parallel to and inside the drawn lines. Proceed to cut the channel with needle files. In this case the best file would be either square or flat with cutting sides.

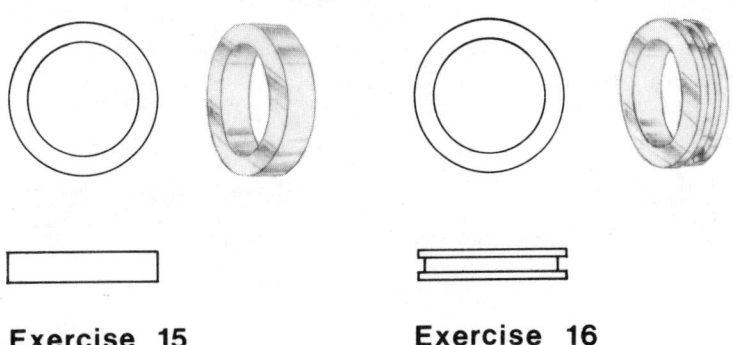

Exercise 15   Exercise 16

EXERCISE 17: Double-Channeled Finger Band

As in the previous exercise, cut channels in the ring. Here there will be two smaller channels, 0.5 mm thick and 1 mm deep, with three raised strips 1 mm wide.

Again, draw lines using the compass, but this time mark only the centers of the two channels, and proceed to cut on them. It would be best to use the saw and then, if available, a knife needle file with a very fine edge.

EXERCISE 18: Concave Finger Band

Here the cutout is concave. It can be from 1 mm to 1.5 mm deep. A rat-tail needle file can be used to begin the cut, and an almond needle file to finish it. The latter has slightly varied curves; use the curve best adapted to the cut.

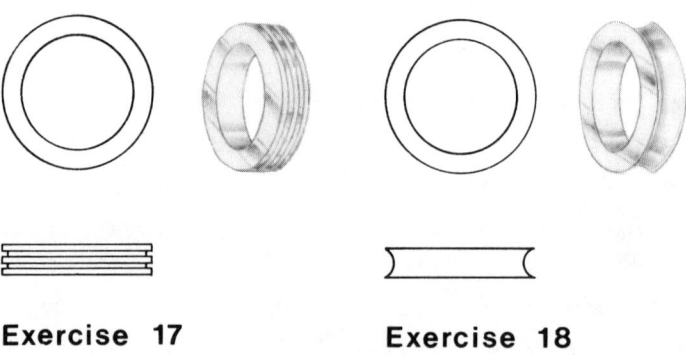

Exercise 17   Exercise 18

EXERCISE 19: Half-Round Finger Band

This is a half-round filing, one of the traditional forms for wedding bands. Beginning with a flat surface, it is easy to arrive at this rounded form. The file to use is 6 in. long, flat or half-round (use the flat side). The curve should begin on the inside edge of the ring and reach the edge on the other side without any facets or intermediate lines.

GOLDSMITHING EXERCISES   37

EXERCISE 20:   **Finger Band with Five Concentric Facets**

This is a five-facet filing. The facets on the top and the two immediately below should be 2mm wide, and those on the sides adjacent to the inside edge of the ring should be 1 mm wide.

Using a compass, draw the two lines of the top part, which will determine the upper central facet, and two lines, one on each side 1 mm from the inside edge of the ring, which will define the two small facets. Then file between the two pairs of lines drawn on each side. It is important that the slopes of the facets be very precise and defined.

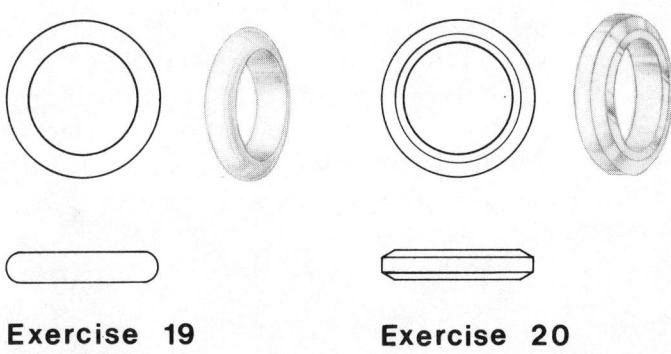

Exercise 19   Exercise 20

EXERCISE 21:   **Finger Band with Twelve Facets**

Although it does not look it, this is the most difficult exercise in the series. It involves twelve equal facets with parallel meeting points.

Draw a circle with a circumference slightly smaller in diameter than the inside of the ring, and a concentric circle quite a bit larger. Using a ruler, steel square, and protractor, or just a compass, divide the larger circle into twelve parts. Once the twelve points of division have been determined, draw straight lines from these points through the center of the circles.

Place the ring on top of the drawing so the first circle is centered inside the ring. Use a marker to indicate the points where the drawn lines meet the metal. Using the square, mark these lines on the metal by drawing very precise lines, all parallel to each other. These will be the meeting lines between the facets.

It is a good idea to file the facets, getting as close as possible to the lines of definition without touching them. Only when you are sure that all the facets are regular and even should you proceed to file to the meeting line between them.

EXERCISE 22: Finger Band with Harlequin Facets

This exercise may seem the most complicated, but it is actually easier than the preceding one. When you have finished a series of facet cuts and begin a second one, the figure begins to take shape by itself. First divide the surface in eight. You can use the same method as in Exercise 21, or approximate it with the compass. File these eight facets until their sides meet. With a compass, draw a central line around the ring, marking the meetings between the facets. Then file on the side of the ring so that the new facet has as its limit the middle of two of the upper facets. This filing will reach the inside edge of the line previously drawn. Do this work on each side of the ring. There will be sixteen facets of this kind per side. Finally, cut the facets which begin from the inside edge of the ring and whose slopes end in the center of the upper facets.

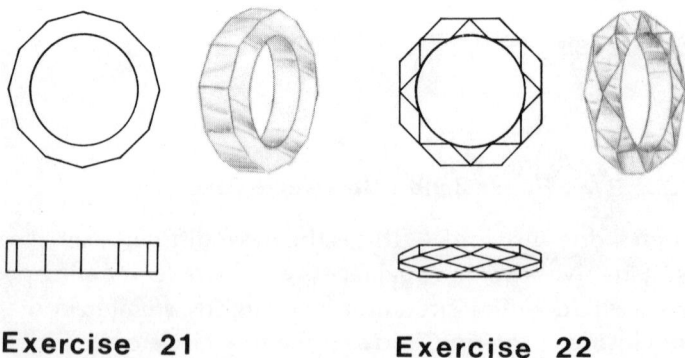

Exercise 21   Exercise 22

EXERCISES 23 THROUGH 27

Objective: Simple bezel fabrication for cabochon and faceted cut stones
Material: Brass, 0.8 mm thick unless otherwise indicated
Scale: 1:1

This series of exercises comprises five types of bezels for faceted and cabochon cut stones. The beginning of the bezel consists of closing the metal around the stone as closely as possible. To do this you will have to make the bezel very close around the stone, but allowing the stone to enter without forcing it.

For a bezel enclosing a round stone, calculate the circumference by multiplying the diameter of the stone by 3.1416 (π) and adding twice the thickness of the metal.

For a bezel enclosing an oval-shaped stone, calculate the circumference by multiplying the sum of half the longer axis and half the shorter axis by 3.1416 (π) and adding twice the thickness of the metal.

EXERCISE 23: Cabochon Setting for Round Stone with Closed Bottom

This is one of the commonest and simplest bezels. The base is usually part of the fabricated piece, to which the bezel is added. Here you will make a bezel à *nuit,* or with the bottom closed.

First calculate the length of metal necessary to enclose the stone (using the method described above) and cut the strip. Calculate the width of the strip according to the angle of the cut of the stone (a). After annealing the metal and filing its ends to a right angle, chamfer the metal slightly along the entire length, using a block with a gutter-shaped channel or an appropriately shaped groove (b). This is important, because if a strip of this width is bent without having been chamfered, the surface tensions in the center will be different from those on the edge, and the edges will be higher than the center. Chamfering slightly so the edges curve in the direction in which the metal will bend allows the surface tensions to remain equal when the strip is bent, resulting in a perfectly flat band.

Bend the metal with a half-round–half-flat pliers (forming pliers) so that the ends meet. If the joint is not perfect, make it as close as possible and cut through the joint with a 0 or 2/0 saw to even up the two sides. Join them and solder. To give it a perfectly round shape, use a bezel mandrel, the same way as for the rings in the previous exercises. Once the bezel is round, file the upper and lower parts, making sure the walls are parallel to each other and perpendicular to the base and top. Solder the base onto one of the sides; the solder can be applied outside or inside. Cut off the excess metal of the base, file all around and sand.

EXERCISE 24: Bezel for a Cabochon Round Stone with Interior Shelf and Open Bottom

The first steps are exactly the same as in the preceding exercise. Instead of soldering the base onto one side, prepare a second ring to be placed inside the first. This will allow the stone to be lifted to a desired height, and the bottom can thus be left open. This allows for greater light if the stone is transparent. To calculate the length needed to make the inside shelf, measure the inside diameter of the bezel and multiply it by 3.1416. It will not be necessary to add the thickness of the metal in this case, as the measurement obtained will be that of the exterior diameter of the interior ring.

EXERCISE 25: Bezel for Cabochon Oval Stone with Interior Shelf and Open Bottom

This exercise is practically the same as the preceding one. Since the stone is oval, the length of the metal must be calculated according to the formula for the circumference of an oval given in the introduction to this series. To make the oval regular, use an oval bezel mandrel. If you don't have the exact form available, adapt or make a tool that will give the desired shape, or use pliers or a small anvil.

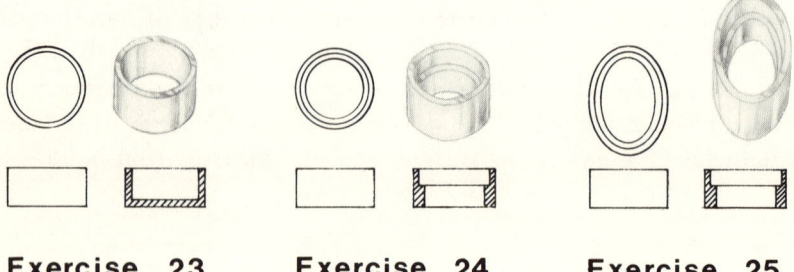

Exercise 23   Exercise 24   Exercise 25

EXERCISE 26:   Conical Bezel

Material: Metal, 1 mm thick

This type of bezel is most often used with faceted stones, although it can also be used with certain types of cabochon stones. The construction of this conical bezel will be the basis for all coronet-type settings.

Layout: Measure the diameter of the stone to be used, and add one thickness of the metal which you will use to make the cone. This will be the upper exterior diameter of the setting. Then determine the height of the setting and the diameter of the lower part, which should have a balanced relation to the upper part. In this exercise, the upper diameter is 11 mm and the lower 8 mm. With these measurements and the height, draw a truncated cone on a piece of paper. With a ruler, project the sides until they meet in a point (a, dotted lines). Using a compass, draw two arcs of about 160°, with the point resting on the intersection of the projected sides and the pencil on the vertices of the sides of the truncated cone (a). Then, with the compass or a ruler, extend the width of the larger end of the cone equally on both sides, and mark two points on the arc. From these new points, draw straight lines to the center of the arc, which is also the meeting point of the lateral lines of the cone (dotted lines). The continued arcs define the dimension and curvature necessary to make the cone according to the specified measurements (a).

Cut out the paper layout and paste it with a good adhesive on the metal with which you will make the bezel. Cut outside the line and file. Repeat all the steps of the previous settings, finding a proper tool for rounding.

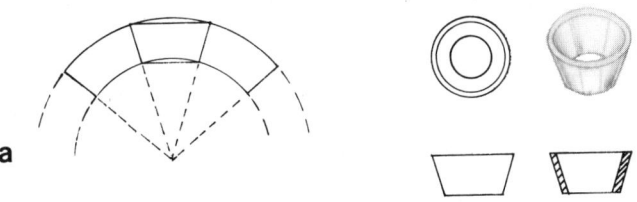

a

EXERCISE 27: Square Bezel (Truncated Pyramid), for Faceted or Cabochon Cut Stone

Material: Metal, four sides of truncated pyramid, 1.2 mm thick; upper square, 0.6 mm

This bezel can be made in two ways. One is to cut the four sides of the truncated pyramid and form them into the proper angles for assembly (a). Place the four parts on a piece of plasticine, the wide part on top, and cover with plaster of Paris or investment for lost wax casting. When this has hardened, remove the plasticine, being careful to clean the joints of the sides well, and proceed to solder the four corners.

The second method is to do the layout on a piece of metal (b) and to proceed exactly as in the exercise for the four-sided pyramid, cutting the corresponding angles in a V shape, and the angles of the four sides. Solder the four joints and then cut out the bottom of the setting (b, dotted lines).

Having used one of the methods described above, make a small bezel to be soldered on the upper (wider) part of the setting. This bezel must be made less thick than the lower part so that the result will be a small shelf on which to rest the stone. In (c) we see the development of the bezel, with its V-shaped sides, 90° in the center and cut at 45° on the ends. The finished bezel is shown in (d).

The final operation is to solder the bezel to the base of the setting, as shown in (e).

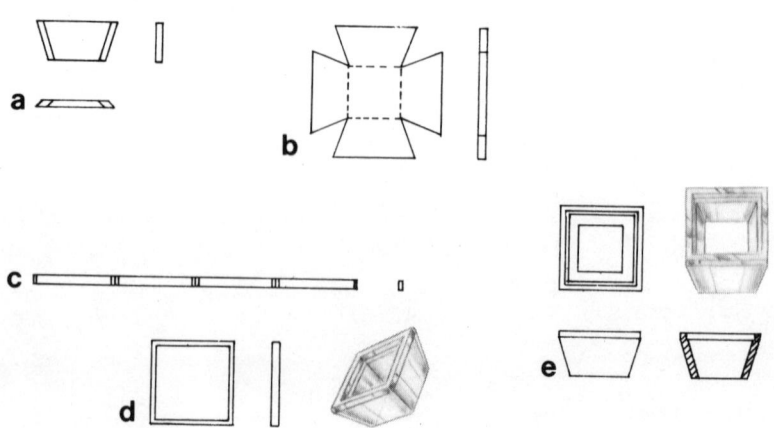

EXERCISE 28: Cuff Links

Metal: Silver; mechanical part of metal, 1.5 mm thick; bridge, 8.5 × 3 × 2.5 mm; button, 0.8 mm thick
Scale: 1:1

This is the first exercise in which a finished piece is made. The objective is to make a pair of cuff links exactly alike. Many of the operations have been previously described, and they will be referred to without further explanation.

Cut two discs of diameter indicated in (a). Emboss them and file around the circumference (b). Cut two discs of the size indicated in (c) and emboss them no deeper than indicated in (d). Cut the tops off the spheres, having first marked the center with a compass and drawn a circle slightly smaller in diameter than that of the two small discs you have already embossed. Place the discs in these openings. File off the angle until it is the opposite of that formed by the embossing. Solder the two small discs inside the openings made in the hemispheres and solder the bases of both, thus closing the pieces completely. File the excess metal and sand the parts. The result is shown in (e); the inside of the button is shown in section.

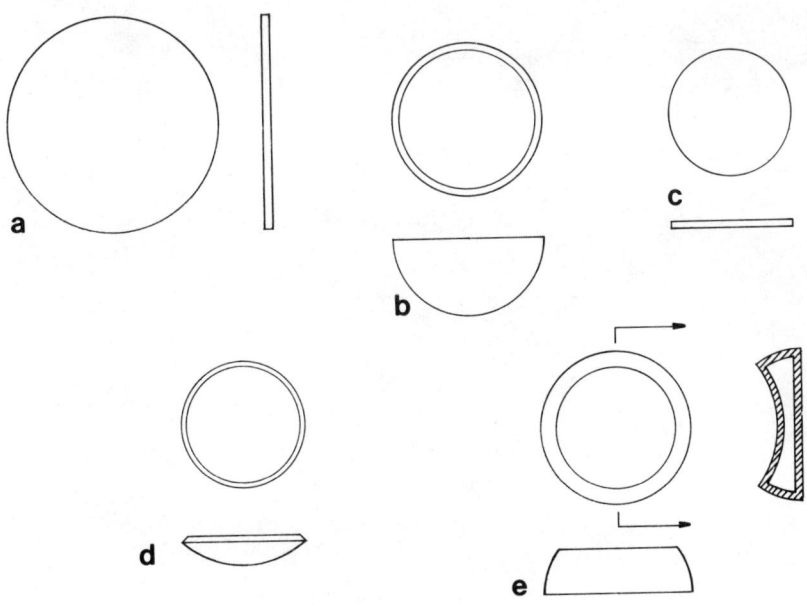

44 THE JEWELER'S CRAFT

Now make the mechanical part. The metal should be thicker, as indicated above. First cut two ellipses (f), then the two bridges on which the system will turn (g), and finally the metal which will join the button to its opposite part, the ellipse (h). Solder these last pieces onto the back of the button. Be careful to place them at the center and on the vertical, as seen when looking at the edge of the metal. Make a small perforation in the center of the back of the button. This hole will be closed by the piece soldered on the back; it serves to avoid building up pressure inside the enclosed space when soldering again. Without it the piece might explode. The last operation is to solder the bridges, making sure to pass them through the opening in the curved pieces which join the button and the ellipse. The final piece is shown in (i).

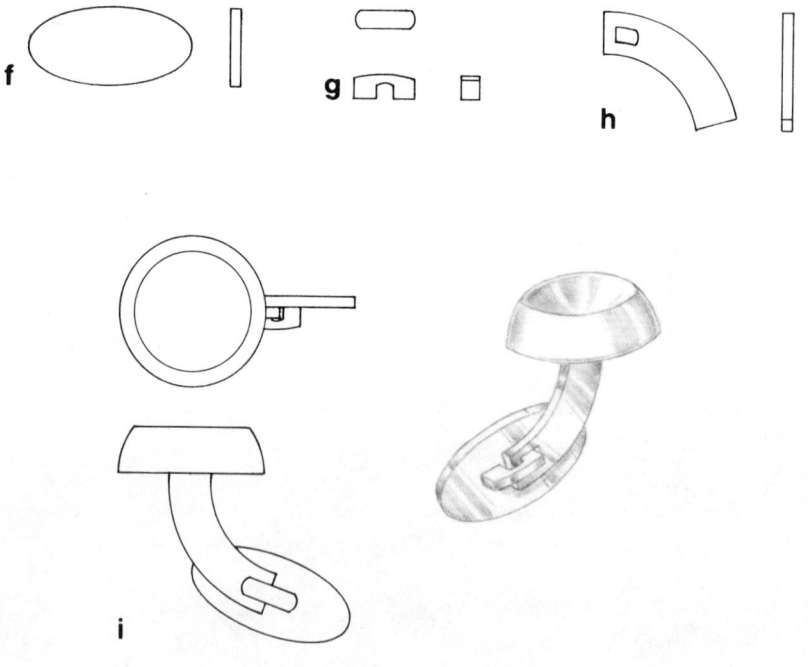

EXERCISE 29: **Box Clasp**

Metal: Silver; top and bottom, 0.6 mm thick; wire for rectangular frame, 0.6 mm × 2.5 mm; final dimension of the box, 7 mm × 11.5 mm × 3.7 mm; part of snap, 0.6 mm in silver 800; metal for back of snap, 1.5 mm × 2.5 mm; presser, 1.5 mm × 3 mm
Scale: 2.1, with the exception of (k), which is drawn to a scale of 1:1.

A clasp of this kind has infinite applications in jewelry. It need not be exactly the same in construction, but the concept will always be the same. When used for a bracelet, for example, the box will be integrated inside one piece of the bracelet.

The cutting of the top and bottom pieces is shown in (a). One of these is the basis for the construction of the system, which is actually the top part of the box. It should be larger than the box itself, as the excess metal will be cut off later on. The measurements can be taken directly from the drawing and reduced to exactly half to achieve the size in (natural) scale 1:1. After cutting the base, make the frame of the box, following the steps described in previous exercises (b). This frame is soldered onto the base (c). Note that it is closer to one side, leaving a shelf for the snap part. Next, cut the keyway for the snap (d).

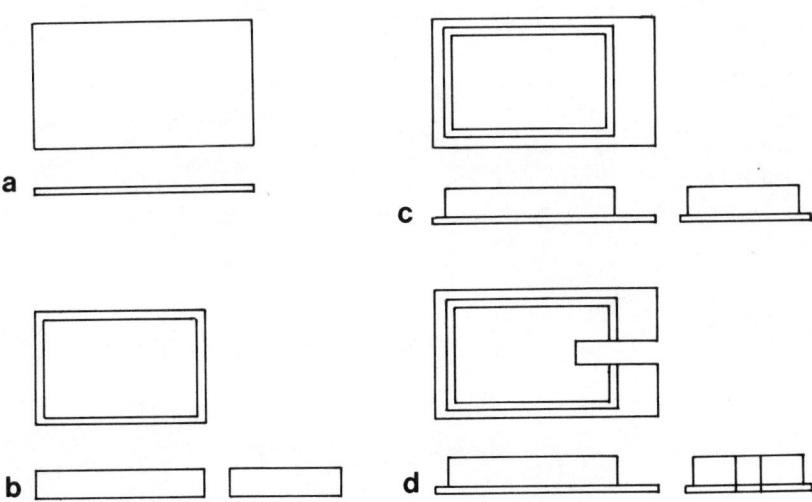

When this part of the box is finished, proceed to make the snap (presser tongue). It should be completely adjusted inside the frame of the box with no lateral play. The measurement derived when constructing the inside of the box will be the measurement of the outside of the snap. The first step is to cut the strip slightly wider than needed and to make an extended V cut (e). The two sides of the cut should be longer than necessary to be able to adjust the parts after bending them. Anneal the metal and then bend it carefully, being careful not to break it. If the V cut is not sufficiently extended and the tongue cannot go further down, do not force it. Cut with a fine saw deeper into the V cut until the top part of the tongue comes down to the height shown in (f) or lower.

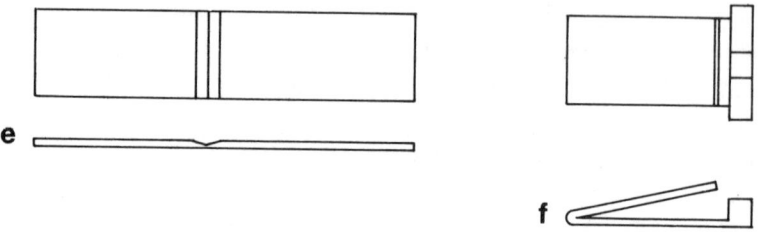

Once the tongue is in this position, solder the joint. Then file the sides of the tongue so that it fits inside the box, and also determine the length of the upper and lower tongues. The upper tongue will snap into the box; the lower tongue will support a bar to be soldered onto it, as shown in (f). The upper part of the tongue should fit exactly inside the frame, facing the point of cutting where the presser will pass. The rear bar of the snap should also have a cut in the center which will allow the presser, when soldered to the upper tongue, to come down as far as possible. Finally, solder the presser (g).

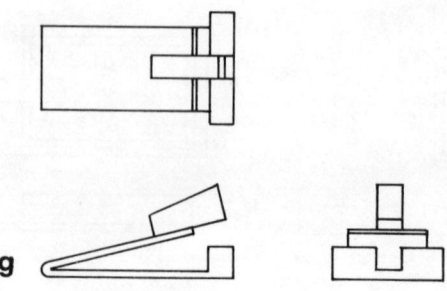

Take the rectangle which was cut at the beginning of the exercise and has not yet been used (a). This will be the lower side of the box. Before soldering it, make a cut in the frame where the presser will enter, of the same width as the snap and deep enough for it to enter, taking into account the thickness of the two tongues. This cut is shown in one of the views of (h). With this cut ready, solder the lower side of the box. File three of the sides until the excess is eliminated on the outside walls of the frame, and file the part of the snap entrance to the height of the rear bar. Nothing but the presser extends beyond the box (i). The details of the interior are shown in (j). In (k) the piece is drawn to scale 1:1 with three views of the orthographic projection.

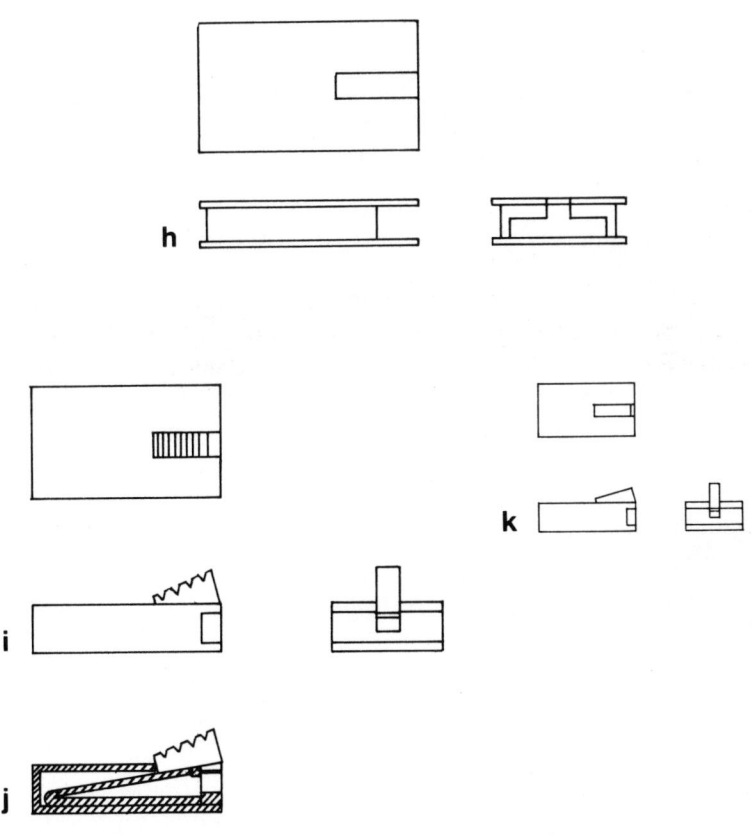

EXERCISE 30: Chain with Square Wire

Metal: silver; square wire, 1.2 mm per side; clasp of sheet, 1 mm thick, 65 cm long
Scale: 1:1

Once you have the square wire, determine the length of the links and cut them all at the same time (a). If square wire is not available, round wire 1.6 mm in diameter can be reduced by drawing it through a square-section drawplate. To determine the length of wire needed, measure the straight part of the link and multiply by two. Add the turn of the two ends, which is calculated by considering the two half-circle turns as a circumference of a circle with diameter equal to the width of the link. Multiply the diameter by 3.1416.

Square wire was chosen for this exercise because it is harder to turn than round wire. When you use pliers to bend a section of square wire, it tends to deform in the bend so that one side is higher than the other. If the operation is done by hand, the deformation is even harder to control.

To make all the links exactly alike, you will have to make a small tool which will be the equivalent of a mandrel used for rings. Take a piece of metal (iron or brass can be used) with a thickness exactly the same as the opening between the parallel wires of the chain, in this case approximately 2 mm. Cut a trapezoidal form whose longer side is only a little longer than the inside of the link and whose shorter side is a little shorter than the inside of the link. The angle of opening should not be very great. The length of the trapezoid can be as shown in (b). Round the two sides of this form carefully with a file. Make sure each curve is a half-circle along the entire length (b).

The ideal place to solder these links is in one of the curves, so that the joint is not noticed should there be any errors. Bend up both ends of each wire with a round-nose pliers to form open hooks about a quarter of the full circumference. In the middle of the wire, make a U-shaped curve so that the two small curves made before meet. Solder the ends of the wire, making them meet exactly. (Another method is to make two U-shaped curves in the wire so that the meeting point falls in the center of one of the sides.

When all the links are ready, give them their final shape, first flattening them and then, using your new tool, giving them all exactly the same opening. It is possible that there will be slight

GOLDSMITHING EXERCISES 49

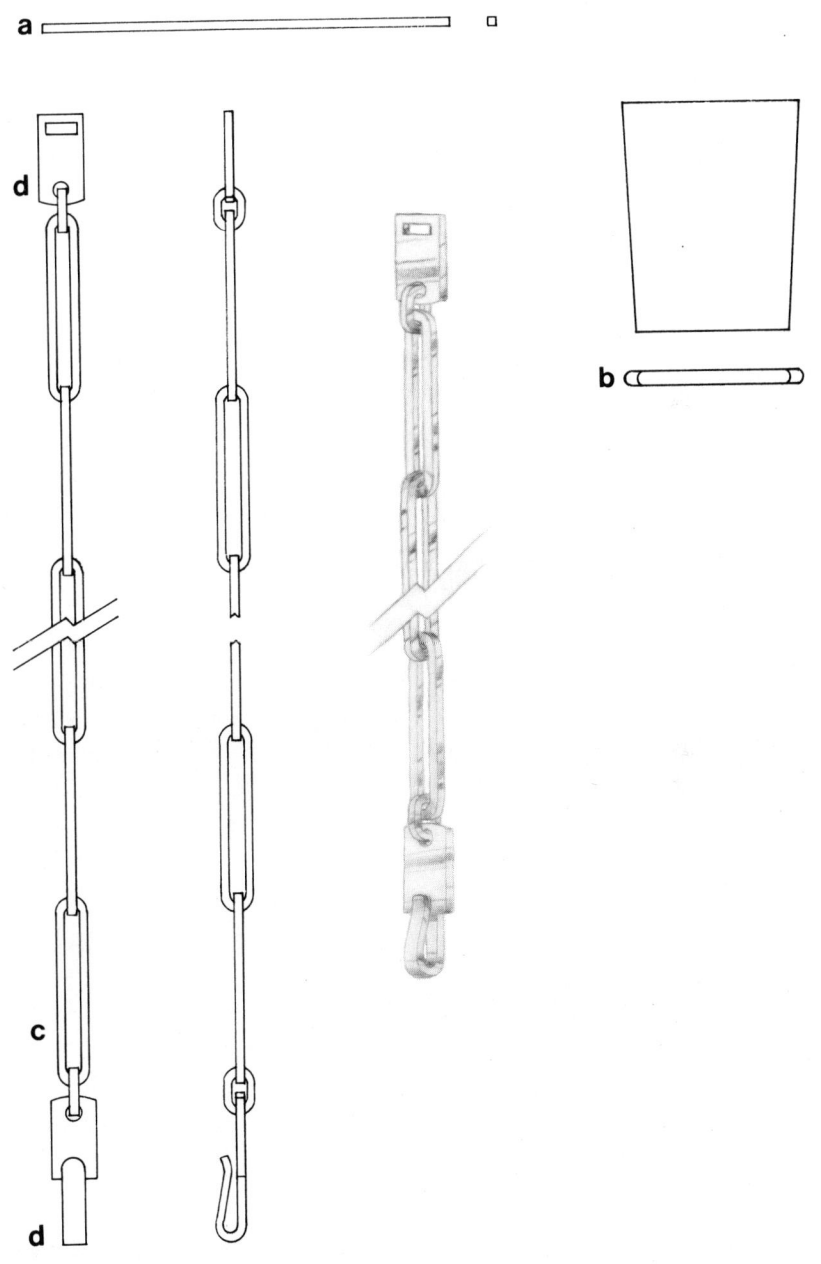

variations in length, but these are not of much importance because they will not be very great. Then sand the links, using sandpaper on a plane and pressing them with your fingers so they slide over the sandpaper.

When all the links are sanded, open half of them on the soldering point to link them. Resolder. If the solder is on the ends, retouch the curve using the same tool. If the solder is on a side, solder a small piece of metal of the same thickness as the cut just made to keep the same length on each side. File off the excess solder and sand. The chain should be as shown in (c), lacking only the clasp.

The clasp is simple (d). Measure the total length of the clasp including the extended hook. Cut a strip of metal the width needed and make the total layout on this strip: width of hook, opening for it on the opposite part, etc. Cut the pieces and form the hook with a round-nose pliers. The two parts of the clasp are joined to the chain by a link of the same wire, sufficiently long to connect the hook and chain.

EXERCISE 31: Locket, Portrait Holder

Metal: silver; front and back of metal, 0.6 mm thick; section of metal of oval frame, 1 mm thick × 5.5 mm wide; exterior hinge, ϕ 2.6, in metal 0.4 mm thick; interior hinge, ϕ 1.75, in metal 0.4 mm thick; catch, 1 mm square wire
Scale: 1:1

The first element to be constructed is the oval frame, which will be the basis for the whole system. You will need a piece of metal 1 mm thick by 5.5 mm wide by 75 mm long, the circumference of the ellipse (a). The length is calculated by multiplying 3.1416 by half of the greater axis plus half of the lesser axis.

$$3.1416 \times (1.35 + 1.05) = 75.5 \text{ mm}$$

Once the metal is cut and the ends filed square, chamfer the metal slightly along the entire length, using a block with a gutter-shaped channel or other appropriately shaped groove (b). This is important, because if a strip of metal of this width is bent without having been chamfered, the surface tensions will be different in the center and along the edges, and the edges end up higher than the center. Chamfering slightly so the edges curve in the direction in which the metal will be bent allows the surface tensions to remain equal when the strip is bent, resulting in a perfectly flat band.

Interestingly, you could use a pair of flat pliers, with a tube whose diameter is slightly less than the shorter axis of the ellipse soldered onto one side of the nose, to support the metal against the tube and thus eliminate the deformation.

Using either system, bend the metal strip, forming, as closely as possible, the required ellipse, being careful to have the joint above one of the ends of the longer axis. Solder it with hard solder. Correct any errors in the curve on a ring mandrel or wooden or metal form similar in shape to the inside of the oval, until you have a perfect ellipse, as shown in (c). Then file the sides, being careful to keep the lines parallel, and tie them for soldering.

Cut two ovals (d), which will be the front and back covers, using the finished frame as a tracing outline. Allow between 0.5 mm and 1 mm extra around the ellipse. After you have filed the edges of the ovals, emboss them on a concave surface or on a dapping block. The ovals will now be slightly convex (e), and if they are placed on a plane, you will see that the center edges do not touch the surface.

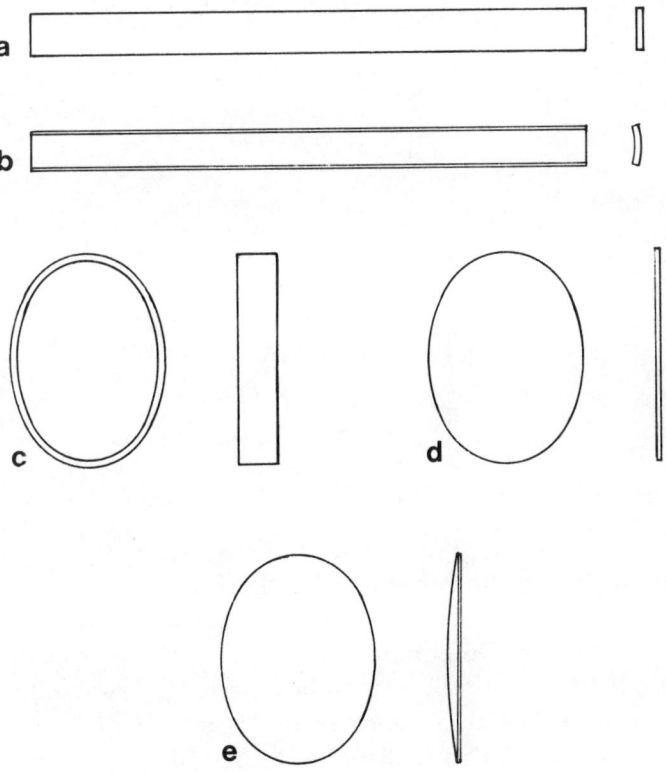

Anneal them and carefully hammer them down until the ellipse is perfectly plane along its circumference. Be especially careful not to allow the ends of the longer axis of the ellipse to rise and so deform the regular convexity of the entire oval. File both covers along the inside edge to have more surface touching the frame.

Solder the two covers with hard solder, file the excess metal, and sand (f). With one leg of a compass placed against the edge of the frame, mark a line around the center of the circumference of the frame. Make four or five perpendicular marks along this line (g) so that, after you have cut the halves, you can place them back in their proper position (h). Cut the halves. File and sand the edges of both halves carefully.

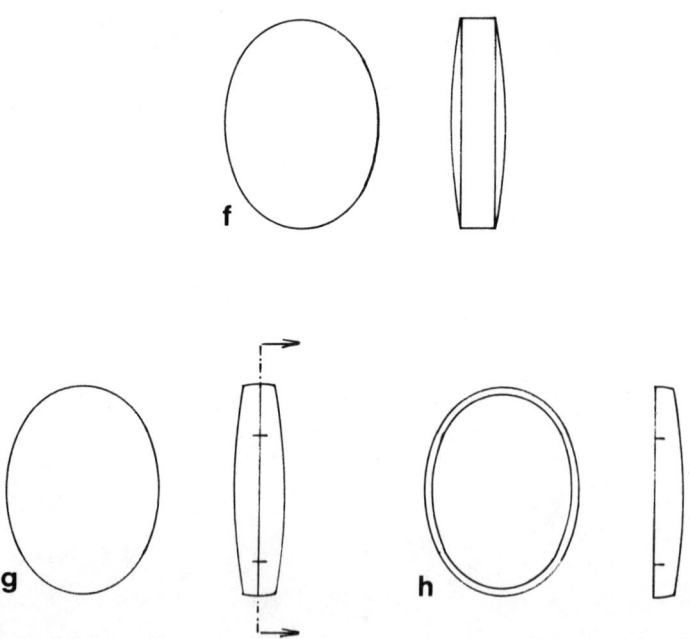

The next step is the preparation of the two tubes for the hinge. One will go inside the other so that there will only be a rotary movement. These tubes can be bought ready-made, but they are simple to construct. Determine the thickness of the walls of both tubes and their exterior diameter. The exterior tube should have a wall 0.4 mm thick with a diameter of 2.6 mm. To calculate the circumference, multiply the diameter by 3.1416.

Exterior tube: 2.6 × 3.1416 = 8.2 mm (approx.)
Interior tube: 1.75 (2.6 less approx. twice the thickness of the wall, 0.85) × 3.1416 = 5.5 (approx.)

Cut two strips of metal approximately 60 mm long by 0.4 mm thick, one 8.2 mm wide for the first tube and the other 5.5 mm wide for the second. The tips should be cut at an angle, as in (i). File both sides carefully and chamfer them, hammering on a design block with appropriately shaped channels until they are almost joined. The more perfect the joint of the tubes, the better the final result will be. Then pass them through a round drawplate until they are uniformly closed. Anneal them and, should the joint open while they are heated, pass them again through the last hole used in the drawplate. Solder the inside tube with hard solder and the outside one with medium or hard solder. With both joints soldered, finish the exterior tube by passing it through the drawplate until it has the diameter required, and then finish the interior tube, drawing it until it fits perfectly inside the exterior one (j). Remember that the more you draw it, the thicker the walls will be.

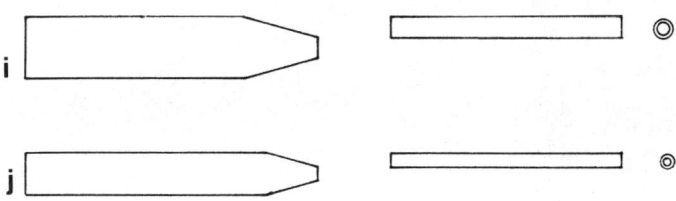

Fill the two halves of the locket with shellac, and heat them until the shellac melts. Be careful not to get shellac on the edges. Put the two faces together and tie them, matching the lines which were made across the circumference line of the frame. Heat the piece again so that the shellac melts and adheres the parts. Make a channel with a rat-tail needle file (k). This should be well centered and parallel to the longer axis of the oval. Make it long and precise enough to support the exterior tube of the hinge according to the measurement indicated. Once the channel is made, separate the two parts by heating the metal. Clean off the shellac with a torch and pickle the piece in a ten-percent solution of sulphuric acid in water. Cut the exterior tube to the length shown in (l).

Before soldering the tube, cut it with a jeweler's saw (#0 or #1) the entire length of the solder. This line should coincide with the joint of the two covers so that, by cutting the exposed side of the tube, you can separate the two parts. Solder the tube to both sides of the locket with medium solder over the channel, tying the walls again so the frames match. Cut five equal and perfectly squared pieces from the second tube, with a combined length equal to that of the first tube. Put these segments inside the first tube (m, left) and affix with a touch of medium or easy solder, alternating three on one side and two on the other. They should be soldered so that the sides of the solder are aligned with the soldered joint of the tubes. Separate the parts and solder them independently. With two pieces of square wire 1 mm thick, make a clasp, soldering one piece to each side of the covers with easy solder, opposite the hinge (m, right). The hinge can be protected with yellow ochre or rouge in order to stop the solder from running along and sealing it. The clasp is made by making a notch 1 mm wide in each wire. Solder a 3 mm piece of the same wire into one of the notches so that it extends far enough to the other side to produce the necessary click of a good clasp. Finally, solder a jump ring on the top center part of the back half, and then make a bail ring, as in (m, upper).

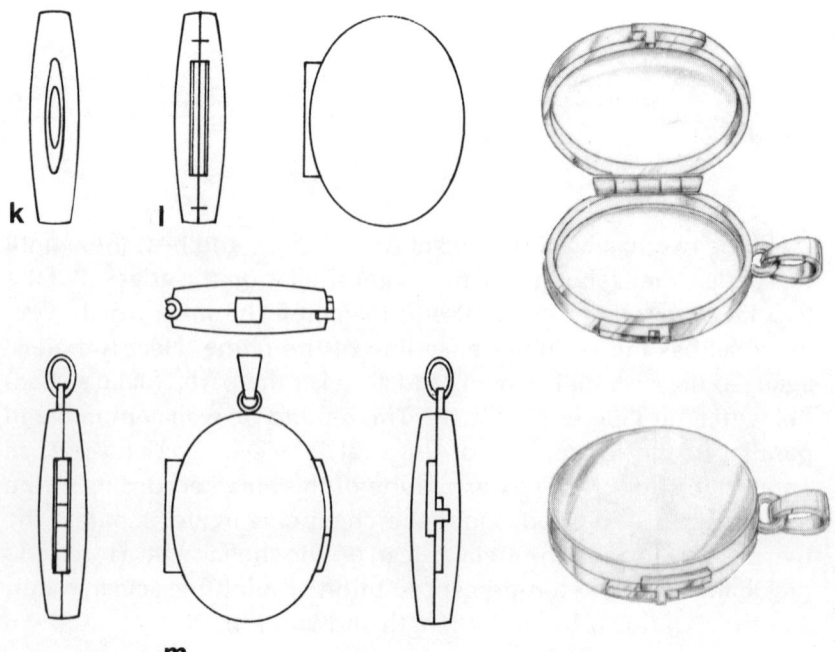

k   l

m

During the process, hold the parts together with either a sewing needle or a steel wire the diameter of the hinge pin, and not with a silver wire, which could easily be soldered to the hinge. Put the final silver pin in after the last soldering and before polishing the piece.

EXERCISE 32: **Simple Round Bracelet**

Metal: sterling silver; band of metal, 1 mm thick; wire for two inside frames, 1.6 mm square; exterior hinge, ϕ 2.8 mm, in metal 0.5 mm thick; interior hinge, ϕ 1.8 mm, in metal 0.4 mm thick; clasp, interior guide in metal 0.4 mm, presser in metal 0.5 mm upper part, 0.6 mm lower part
Scale: 1:1

This is the last of the exercises without stones. Technically, it has several steps similar to those in the preceding exercise. The preparation of the band and the hinge are exactly the same. The box catch, although the beginning is the same as in Exercise 29, is a little different in fabrication. This system is used when there is not enough interior space to sufficiently hide the catch.

Determine the length of the band using the diameter of the exterior circle in (c), the exterior diameter of the bracelet. The width is given in (a); the broken line in the center of (a) indicates a lack of sufficient space to show the entire length of the band. If you wish a narrower or wider bracelet, determine the length of the band with the desired diameter. The standard diameter of a bracelet is between 5.5 and 6 cm. The circumference will be about 18 cm. These figures are the same for movable-parts bracelets.

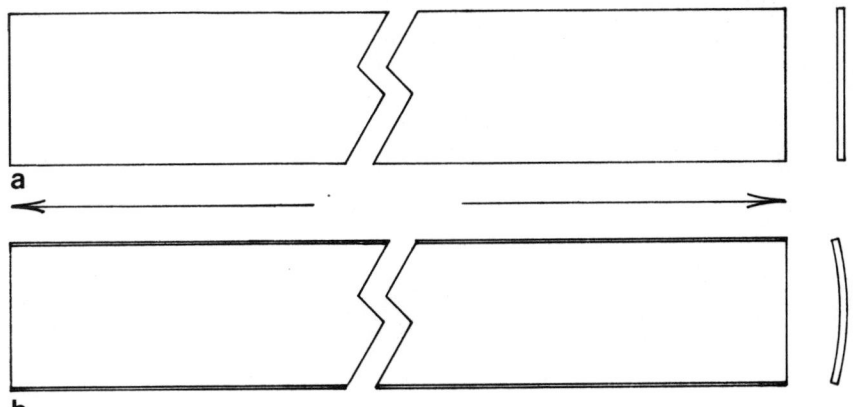

56 THE JEWELER'S CRAFT

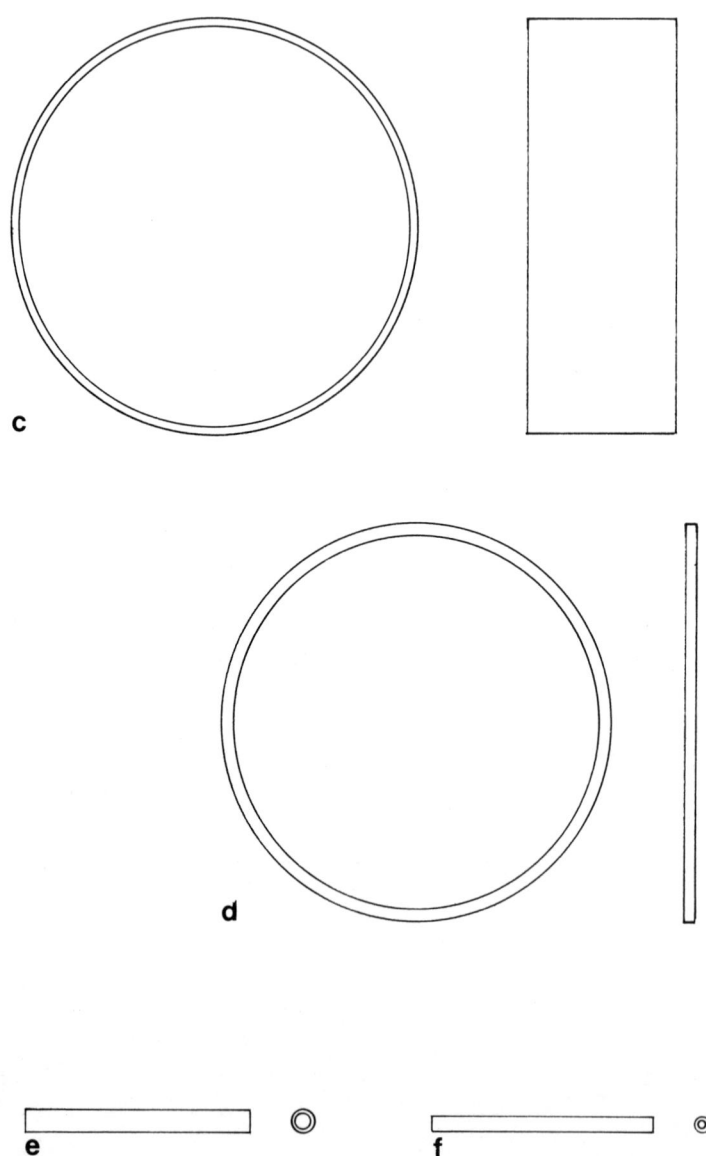

Before forming the band, chamfer the metal as described in Exercise 31 (b). Bend the metal and solder. Using a round bracelet mandrel, give it a round form (c).

Proceed to make the rings, or inside frames, to be soldered on both sides of the bracelet, aligning their solder points with that of the band. These rings have the function of giving consistency, both physical and visual, to the band. Determine the length of the wires by measuring the interior diameter of the band. Cut, bend and make them round using the same bracelet mandrel (d). Prepare for soldering, placing the ring inside the band, leaving a small border toward the outside where the solder will go. Solder and file off the excess metal on both sides.

Make two tubes for the hinge, following the specifications given above and the process detailed in Exercise 31. The tubes should fit exactly inside each other (e and f).

Taking the exterior tube, make a perforation on the solder point of the rings or interior frame, being sure that both are perfectly vertical to each other. Cut the band on the same point and adjust the perforation so that it is perfectly round and the exterior tube of the hinge fits perfectly inside it. You should not have to force it in; forcing it would make the diameter larger than that of the bracelet (g). Once this is adjusted, solder the tube with hard solder, keeping the solder line toward the outside.

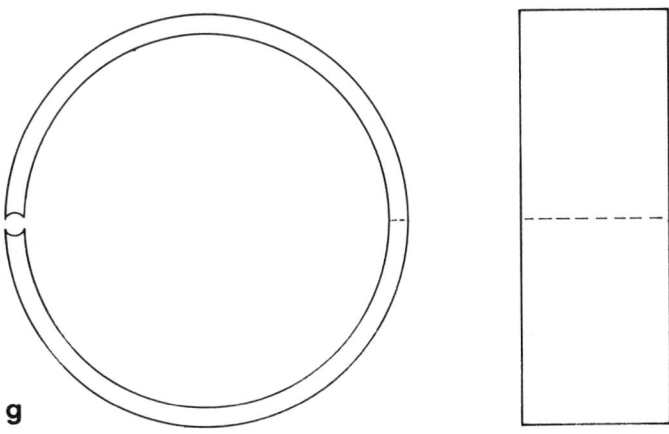

g

Cut the bracelet into exactly equal halves, making sure the cuts are perfectly parallel and, of course, perpendicular to the sides of the bracelet (g, dotted lines). One of the two cuts should be at the exact center of the tube you just soldered. File both sides carefully without removing any excess metal. Finish the hinge as described in the preceding exercise.

On each part of the sides of the clasp, solder a bar of the same metal used for the interior border of the sides of the band. Solder them so they are flush with the edges you just filed.

To make the clasp, first cut the lower tongue (0.6 mm thick, 8 mm wide). This tongue should be cut quite a bit longer than the keyway into which it will slide (h). The tongue is shown in the lower part of (i). To make the keyway, cut a piece of metal slightly longer than the keyway, wide enough to bend around both sides of the tongue (h), and of the thickness indicated at the beginning of the exercise. Bend the metal over the tongue (h, right) and cut it the same length. The upper opening should be very slightly wider than the width of the upper tongue of the clasp where the presser goes. Cut a piece for the upper part of the clasp, with a length as in (i) and a width the same or slightly smaller than that of the upper opening of the keyway. Cut angles at one end of the lower and upper tongue so that when soldered it looks like (i, lower) and solder both, using medium solder.

On the two ends of the bracelet, and on the bars soldered on the band before the clasp was begun, cut out a form so that the keyway fits as low as possible. Also, make a groove for the presser, as shown in (j). Solder the keyway to the two ends of the bracelet on the clasp side. It is important to leave a minimal separation between the two parts, not only so they are not soldered together, but also to be able to introduce a fine saw and to cut the keyway in two. The longer part of the keyway will hold the opening for the presser and in which the clasp will go. The short part serves as a center to solder the lower tongue of the clasp. The adjustment of the clasp should be done as described in Exercise 29. It should be done with the hinge mounted and with a needle or steel (not silver) wire used as an axis. When the clasp is working precisely, mark it across the opening left for the presser, where it will be soldered. This is the last operation in making the bracelet. File and polish, still using a provisional pin on the hinge. The final pin will be inserted just before the final polish. The details of the interior of the bracelet are shown in (k).

GOLDSMITHING EXERCISES

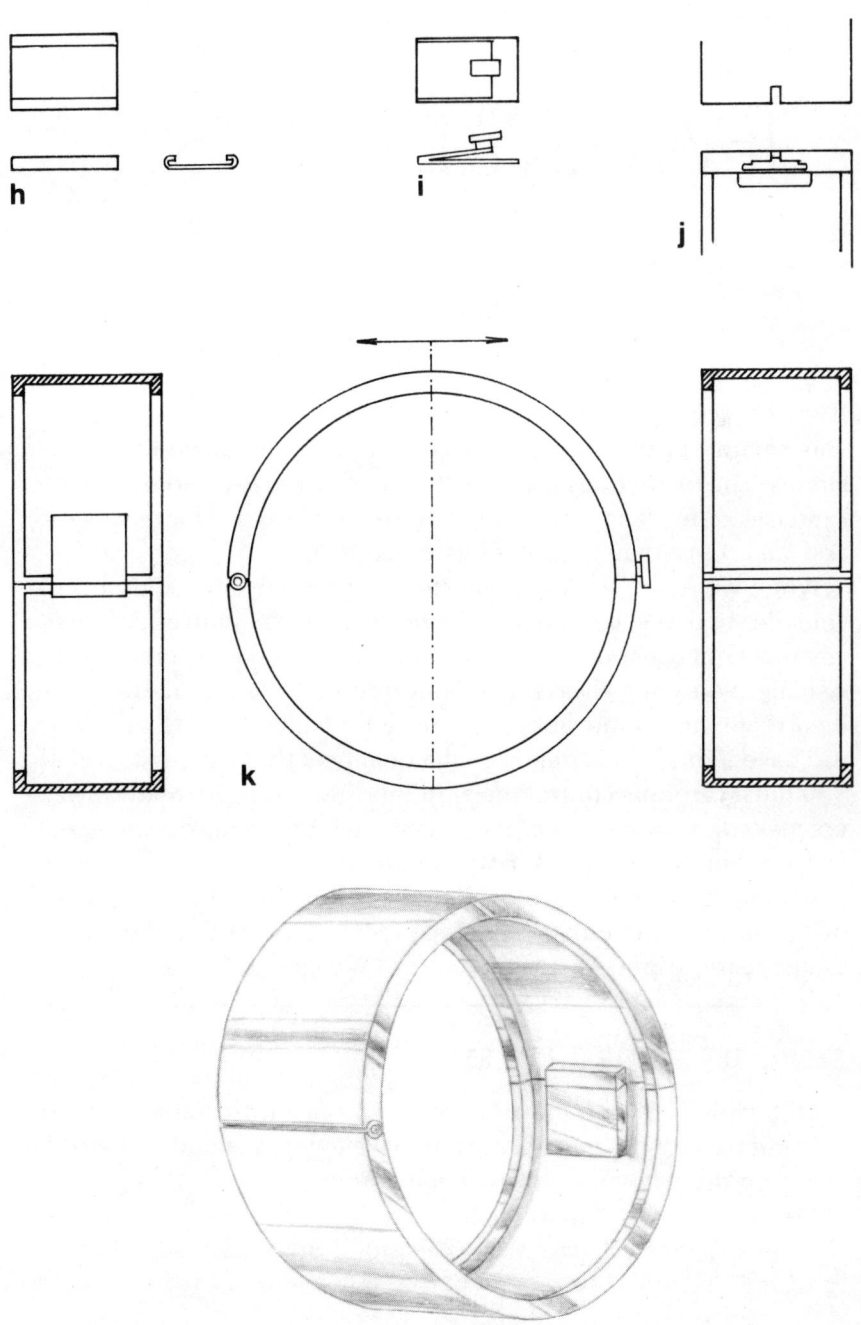

JEWELRY EXERCISES

This section deals only with pieces that include faceted precious stones. The techniques used are the same as those in Goldsmithing Exercises. The steps involved for these exercises are more specific and vary more than the previous ones.

When working with precious stones there are several points to consider so that you ensure the stones have a maximun effect. First, you must not use too much metal, so as not to make the piece heavy visually. You must always take light into consideration. The more light that reaches the stone, the more brilliance and life the stone will have. (This also depends on the quality of the stone and its cut.) You must carefully control the amount of solder used. Many jewelers make the soldering points much heavier than necessary, especially when working with wire. The piece must be perfectly polished, inside and out, including the insides of the settings when possible. And, of course, the piece must be constructed with the utmost care, especially in symmetrical designs.

EXERCISES 33 THROUGH 35

Objective: Distribution of faceted stones on diverse surfaces using flat-top or plate setting and pavé technique and light opening on the back part of the metal (à jour)
Metal: Brass, 1.5 mm thick
Stones: Faceted glass stones as indicated in each exercise
Scale: 1:1

These exercises are for working with stones and their most common settings.

In the first three exercises, a minimum of practice will be given so as to understand the techniques of flat-top or plate setting and pavé setting. This consists of distributing as many stones as necessary on different surfaces until they are covered as much as possible. In many cases, the size of the stones is not the same, as in Exercise 35. The setting and engraving on metal will give the impression of one large stone covering the surface.

One of the important points in this technique is maintaining exactly the same separation between the stones. Normally, 1 mm between stones is considered a good distance for flat-top setting, and 0.5 mm between stones for pavé-set stones and the edges of the metal. This distance is given when the opening in the metal for the stones corresponds to the total diameter, or girdle, of the stone.

The seat for the stone is usually made with a conical bur cutting the metal, until the stone sits with the girdle flush with the metal. The setter's job is to deepen the cut and affix the stone.

The standard steps are first to make the perforations on the points where the stones will go, having first distributed the spaces properly. It is not always possible to make the perforations in the exact places and to leave equal distances between them. Sometimes they slip a bit. For this reason the perforations must be made with bits that are much smaller than the diameter of the stones. Once the perforations are made, proceed to center them and distribute the distances, using a flexible shaft and a cross-cut cone-square bur. You will have to keep controlling the distances, putting the stones on the perforations as they get larger. If the stones are of varying size—even if they are small—you will have to put them on a box with wax or plasticine to keep them in order the whole time and make them coincide with their respective perforations. When the holes are centered, open them with a conical bur. Do not lower them all at once in the beginning; first open the lights on the rear part of the metal with a saw, and then finish by lowering the seats of the stones. The opening of lights on the rear of the metal enables more light to enter at the base of the stone. This is especially effective for pins and pendants.

The process will become clearer during the execution of the following exercises.

EXERCISE 33: Flat-Top or Plate Setting on a Straight Plane

Stones: 3.8 mm to 4 mm in diameter

In this case you will need stones of equal, or nearly equal, size. First cut the bar on which the stones will be set (a). The dimension of this bar is determined by the size and quantity of the stones. The distance between the stones should be from 0.5 mm to 1 mm, and the distance between the stones and the edges of the metal is 0.5 mm.

Open the perforations, having first determined the distances between stones (b). Then, using a cross-cut cone-square bur, center them properly. Using a conical bur, open the perforations which are not already of the diameter of the stones. Open the lights on the rear part of the metal with a 2/0 saw (approximately); (c) shows lights openings for each stone. These openings are usually square. Leave 0.5 mm to 1 mm distance between each of them according to the distance left between stones, and 0.5 mm between the stones and the edge of the metal. As the cut is square and somewhat angled toward the center, make four precise angles on the vertices of the square. The proportion of the cut between the seat and the stone and the lights is shown, in enlarged scale, in (d). Once the light openings are finished, proceed to retouch the seat of the stones on the upper surface. The finished work is shown in (e).

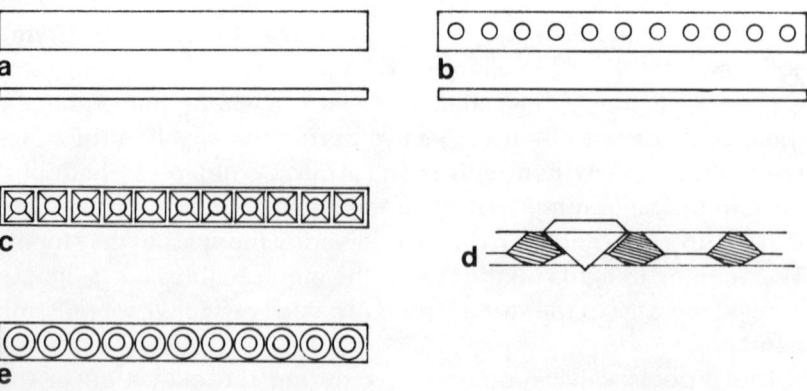

EXERCISE 34: Flat-Top or Plate Setting on Curved Plane

Stones: 2.8 mm to 3 mm in diameter

The steps are exactly the same as those in the preceding exercise. The only difference is the closed curve or circle, which has no beginning or end and whose lights are slightly trapezoidal rather than square. The distribution will be a little more difficult than in Exercise 33. In (a) we have the ring in metal; (b) shows the seats for the stones; (c) shows the lights.

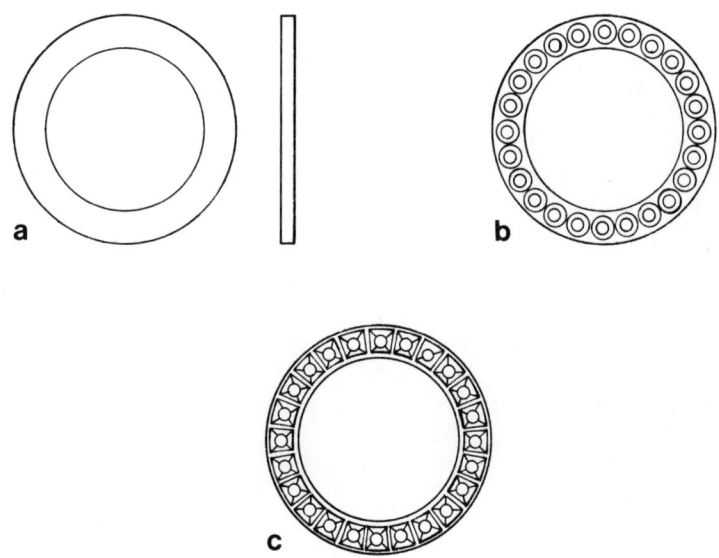

EXERCISE 35: Pavé Setting on a Hemisphere

Stones: various sizes

First cut a circle of metal and emboss it until you have a hemisphere. Remember that when embossing a disc, the diameter of the sphere will be approximately 20 to 25 percent less than the diameter of the flat disc. This will depend on the thickness of the metal and the manner of embossing it.

Once the hemisphere is done, distribute the stones, beginning at the point of greatest diameter. It is more difficult to perforate on a convex surface than on a plane. Before drilling a hole, mark with a center punch so the bit will not slip. Also, drill in a perfectly perpendicular line to the tangent of the sphere.

The last stones to be set are those on the upper part. The stones should be measured one by one. Make the perforation for a stone, then center it if you need to, enlarge it, place the stone on it, and measure for another stone to be placed beside it. Preferably, you should put stones of equal size on the first line around the base (the greatest diameter) and distribute them equally.

The light work will be same as in the other exercises, with the difference that in this case you will be working on a concave surface and inside the hemisphere. In (a), the form of distribution is shown; (b) shows the light in the inside of the hemisphere; the details, in enlarged scale (c) and (d), show two forms of distribution of the stones on the surface. The hexagonally shaped lights are shown enlarged in (e).

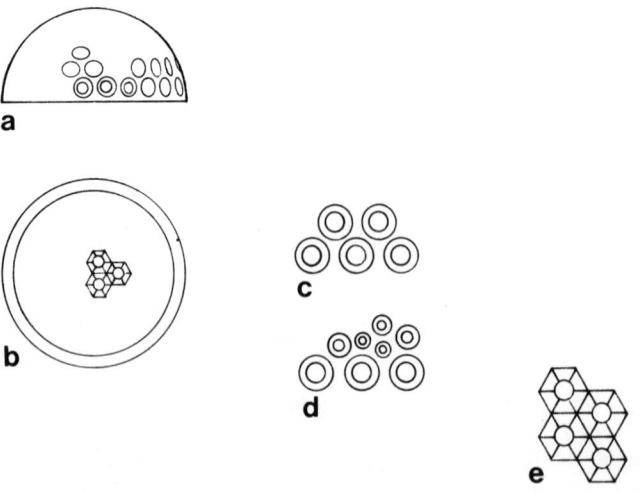

JEWELRY EXERCISES

EXERCISES 36 THROUGH 38

Objective: Application of the previous exercises—fabrication of a ring and two pins

Metal: Silver; ring with rectangular section of 2.2 mm × 4 mm; pins with upper part in metal 1.3 mm thick, lower frame in metal 1 mm thick, bridges in round wire φ 1.2 mm

Scale 1:1

EXERCISE 36: Eternity Band with Stones

Stones: 3 mm in diameter

Make a ring of any dimension, taking into consideration the width and thickness specified above. Once it is made, draw a line around the center of the exterior surface. On this line, make the centers for distribution of the stones (a). The rest of the work is exactly the same as in the previous exercises; (b) shows the seats of the stones, and (c) shows the detail, in enlarged scale, of the lights on the inside. Making the lights on the inside of the ring is the most complicated undertaking up to now.

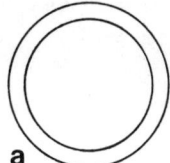
a

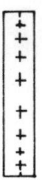
b

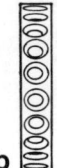

c

EXERCISE 37: Pin with Stones

Stones: 3.5 mm to 4 mm in diameter

This pin is an application of Exercise 33. Determine its measurements according to the type of stones to be used. Remember to leave from 0.5 mm to 1 mm between the stones and 0.5 mm between the stones and the edge of the metal. The drawings of the exercise are to be used only as reference.

Once the upper part is done with its respective lights (a), make the lower frame with an exterior measurement exactly that of the upper part. This frame can be made of square wire section 1 mm per side or, better, by cutting the inside and outside of a piece of sheet 1 mm thick (b).

Prepare round wire 1.2 mm in diameter. This will be used to make the bridges of separation between the upper and lower parts. The reason for these two parts is to give greater physical and visual consistency to the piece. Also, having the two sides open allows more light to enter at the base of the stones.

Cut pieces of wire slightly longer than the width of the piece. These are to be tied from one side of the frame to the other (determine the distance between them beforehand). You can put as many as shown in (c), or place one between each stone so as to give greater symmetry in relation to the stones. For the corners, make angles with a V cut in the wire. Tie all the wires and solder them on the frame (c). Cut the inside part of the wires in the frame, file and sand.

Solder the upper and lower parts, and file the excess of the wires. The piece is shown from one side in (d).

The body of the pin is now done. You only need to attach the pin and pin catch. It is recommended, just for practice, to make the entire pin part. This work is not normally done by hand, as various types and qualities of pins are found on the market. The description of the technique is at the end of the series of exercises with faceted stones.

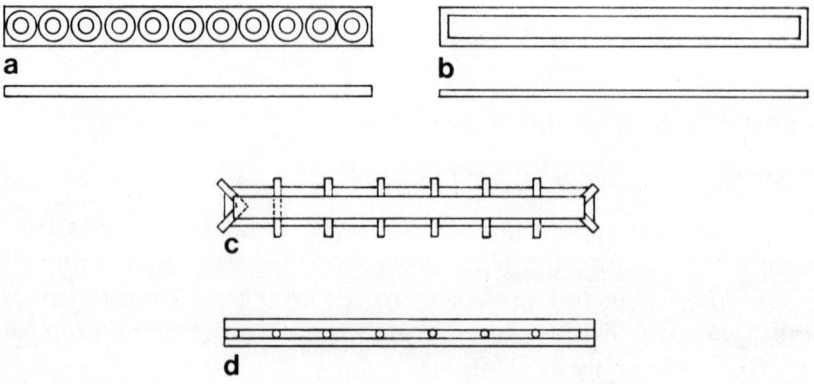

EXERCISE 38: Pin with Stones

Stones: ϕ6 mm, ϕ5 mm, ϕ4.5 or ϕ4 mm, ϕ4 or ϕ3.5 mm, ϕ3.5 or ϕ3 mm; the stones are in pairs decreasing in size

This variation on the previous exercise consists of the pin's having not a straight edge but diminishing curves, from the center to the ends. The main difference in construction comes from the fact that you must begin to distribute the stones and to make their seats before cutting the metal.

Draw a straight line on a piece of metal of the given thickness. The centers of the stones will be on this line. Begin with the center stone; perforate the center and seat the central stone as described. Then seat the two lateral stones, one on each side, and continue until reaching the ends. Maintain the distance of 0.5 mm to 1 mm between stones. If the stones are very large, this distance could grow as well. When all the stones are seated, proceed to cut the outside of the pin. Mark half-circles with the compass on both sides of the stones. The two ends will be nearly a complete circle. Cut the outside and file, being careful that the metal is consistently wide between the stone and the edge (a). The light openings will be made directly with the conical bur.

The rest of the work is the same as described in the preceding exercise. Cut the rear part, beginning with a sheet 1 mm thick, using the upper part as a guide (b), and then mount it with bridges of round wire. The position of these bridges is shown in (c).

Again, it is advisable to make the pin part by hand.

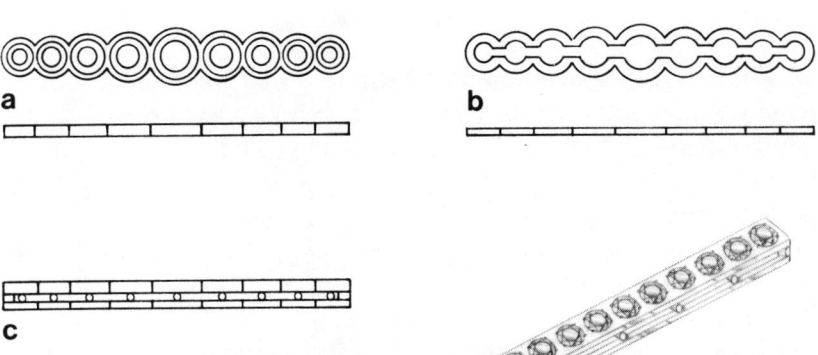

EXERCISE 39: Crown Setting with Six Prongs

Metal: Brass; cone, 1 mm thick; base wire, 1.25 mm thick per side; dimensions of cone, ϕ 12 mm for upper part, ϕ 7.5 mm for lower part
Scale: 2:1 for construction steps, 1:1 for final piece

The construction of this setting is the basis for the construction of any conical setting with prongs. This exercise uses a rather large setting in order to offer a clearer understanding of the process, and also because a piece of such difficulty would not be easily undertaken by a beginner in a smaller size.

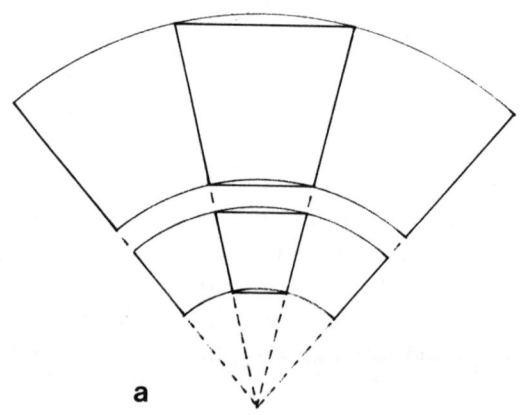

a

Although the description of the formation of a cone has already been given, it will not hurt to repeat it. In (a) we have the development in scales 2:1 and 1:1; the second is used for the setting. Take the measurements from the 2:1 scale and divide by two. All the work must be constantly checked for correct measurements.

The first step is to specify the measurements of the cone and to draw it on a piece of paper. In this case we have an upper diameter of 12 mm and a lower diameter of 7.5 mm, with a height of 11 mm. Having drawn the cone's final dimension, project its sides from the wider part toward the narrower, until the lines meet at a point, as shown by the inside dotted lines in (a). Resting the compass point on this point and with the leg open to rest on one of the upper angles of the cone, draw a curve long enough for the upper measurement of the cone to fit in it three times. Repeat the operation, closing the compass to rest on the lower angle of the cone. With a ruler or the compass, measure the width on the cone and mark its equivalent on each side arc. Project two lines to meet at the center point of the first projection. The resulting shape, drawn inside the two arcs and the two last projections, is the form and dimension of the metal you need to make the cone.

Once the cone is made and adjusted on a bezel mandrel or bezel block (b), proceed to make the cuts for the lower openings and for the prongs. The joining line of the cone should never be on any of the prongs. In this exercise it will be on one of the points of the base of the cone. First make the cuts for the lower openings. These will have an ogival shape—that of a pointed, or Gothic, arch (c). It is important to create symmetry in these points. To make them, use the compass and any instrument that will allow you to make a precise outline. The depth of the cut should be slightly less than half the height of the cone. Once you have made the cuts with a saw, proceed to even them with a triangle needle file.

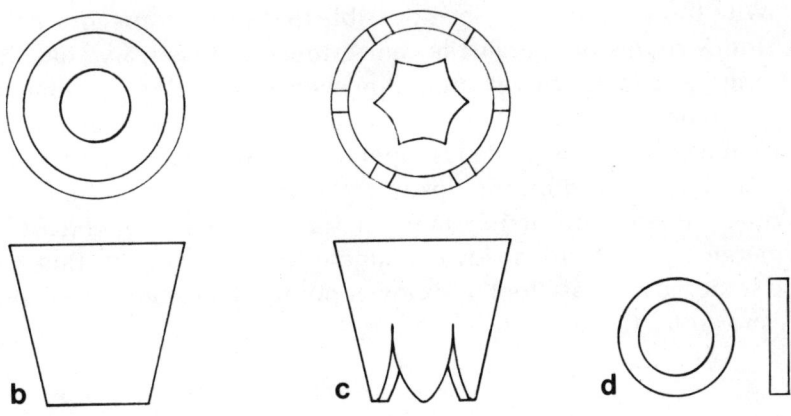

Now make the prongs. You will also have to distribute these proportionately. The division is again in six parts. The lower curve, toward the center of the cone, should be slightly lower than the vertical center of the cone and centered between the ogival arches (e).

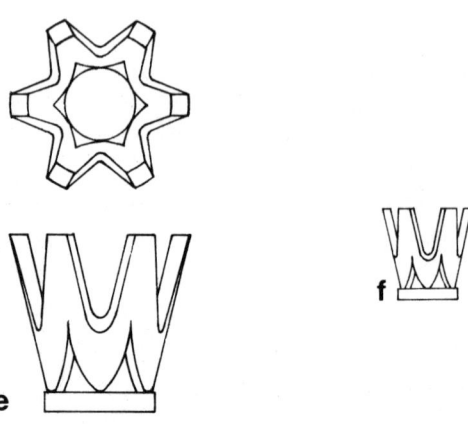

With the saw, cut as close as possible to the marks already made. Using a round or rat-tail file, and others as necessary, file the prongs. The lower curves should be even and exactly the same, as should the widths of the tips. The entire work should be harmonious in its proportions. The last operation is to make the lower ring (d), to be soldered on the tips of the narrowest part of the cone. With a square wire of 1.25 mm per side, make a ring which will emerge slightly from the lower diameter of the cone. This ring will be soldered as a base for the six lower points of the cone. The result is shown in (f).

JEWELRY EXERCISES 71

EXERCISES 40 AND 41

Objective: Rings with four-prong and six-prong crown settings
Metal: Silver; for settings, 1.2 mm thick; shank metal, 3.5 mm wide × 2.5 mm thick for Exercise 40 and 2 mm thick for Exercise 41.
Scale: 1:1

There is a great variety of crown settings, among which those presented in these exercises are fairly common. In order to practice different divisions of the cone, one four- and one six-prong setting have been chosen, and the shanks are also different. One is forged and the other is cut and filed. The cones are exactly alike and the construction of them is that previously given.

EXERCISE 40: Ring with Four-Prong Crown Setting and Knife-Edge Shank

Beginning with the cone (a), measure the length of the prongs and divide the upper part in four. The measurements may be taken directly from (b), reducing them in half. Remember to make the cuts so that the seam of the cone does not fall in any of the prongs. Once the four prongs are cut and filed, make one channel in each prong along its length and reaching the base of the cone. This channel goes over the top part of the prong.

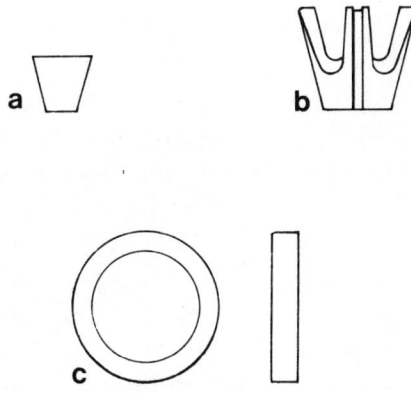

Follow the technical specifications given for the ring, making it to any ring size and in accordance with (c). With a hammer, preferably a forge hammer, expand the part of the shank where the solder will go, as seen in (d). With sufficient material to cut the form of the shank (e), file the lateral surfaces of the ring so that it is about 3 mm at the base and 1 mm at the upper part. Draw the angle of the cone and cut and file as in (e). On the lower part of the setting, make an arc toward the inside, approximately the same as the curvature of the inside of the ring. Bear in mind that the setting will be soldered to the ring at the prongs and not at the cut between the prongs.

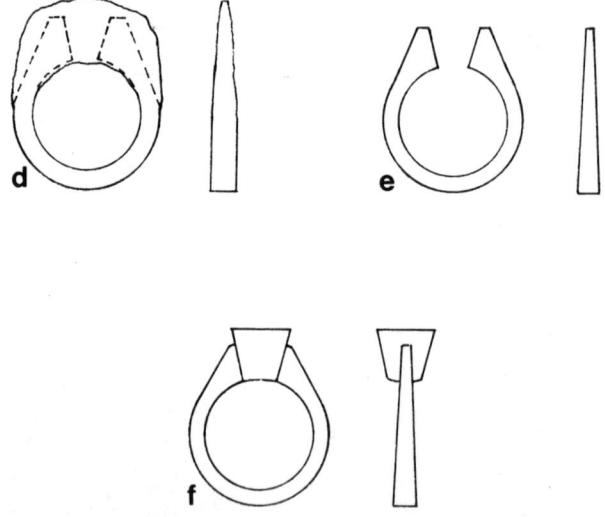

The finished ring is shown with the setting outlined in (f). To solder the setting on the ring, tie it with wrapping wire or annealed black iron wire. First tack the setting on one side and confirm its position. If it is correctly placed, solder the opposite side and then the tacked side. If the setting is not properly centered when tacked, correct it by turning it or simply taking it off and repeating the operation from the beginning. File the inside of the ring with a rotary file or with a rubber wheel at the soldering of the setting. Sand.

EXERCISE 41: Ring with Six-Prong Crown Setting

Beginning with the cone (a), make the necessary cuts for six prongs (b). The shank is different from that in Exercise 40. The first step (c) is the same, with different measurements for the shank. With a compass, make a line in the center of both sides long enough to allow the supports of the setting to be cut from it. This line should be above the soldering area since, when the ring is opened, you will cut on the solder. Cut on the solder, and also cut on the lines drawn on both sides of the ring.

When these cuts are made, bend the sides of the upper part of the cut as shown in (d), and file the sides of the shank so that the lower part is about 3 mm wide and the upper part is about 1 mm wide. As the ring is open, it is very easy to change the measurement while filing, making it either larger or smaller. Before soldering the setting, adjust the angles of the four supports of the shank, making sure the setting is centered and vertical. Tie, as in the previous exercise, and tack one of the lower supports. Repeat the checking operation, correct if necessary, and finally solder the four supports. The inside curve of the ring, where the setting is soldered, should be corrected by filing, as explained in Exercise 40.

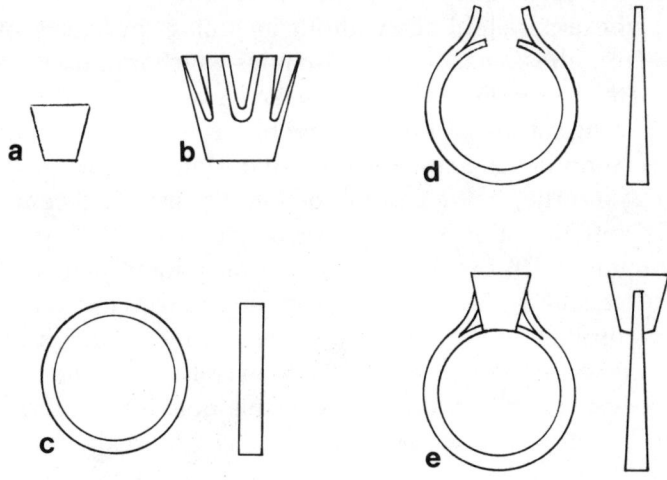

EXERCISE 42: Ring with Box-Frame Setting

Metal: Silver; setting, 0.8 mm thick; prongs, 0.9 mm thick; shank, 5 mm wide, 1.5 mm thick
Stone: Emerald-cut stone, 20 mm × 14 mm
Scale: 1:1

Again, a rather large stone has been chosen to facilitate constructing this ring. The measurements to be considered in making any box setting are the width and length of the stone to be used. The height of the setting depends on the height of the stone and also on a graceful proportion among the parts.

On a piece of metal (a), draw the layout of the sides of the setting. There are three important measurements to be considered: the total length and width of the stone, the length of its straight sides without taking into account the angles of the corners, and the height of the stone from its girdle to the lowest point of the base. The layout begins with the drawing of a rectangle (b, dotted lines) in the center of the figure. This rectangle, together with the height you have decided upon, will determine the lateral angles of the setting. If it is very narrow, the angle will be more pronounced; if wide, the result will be just the opposite. From the four sides of this rectangle, mark the lengths of the side walls of the setting and draw lines parallel to the rectangle. Determine the length of the sides of the stone on these parallel lines without including the facets of the corners. From these marks, draw the lines which join them to the vertices of the rectangle. You will now have a layout as in (b); in this case, a drawing was made for a narrow-based setting. If you want a wider one, simply change the relations of the initial rectangle. Once drawn, cut and file, being careful to keep the measurements.

On the dotted line of the inside rectangle, make V-shaped cuts with an engraver. These cuts will be the turning points of the walls of the box. Close these walls until the stone is seated on the four sides, being careful that all the angles are equal. Looking down on the stone, a minimal line of metal should show, part of the metal being under the stone. Solder the angles of this opening; the result is shown in (c). File the upper part of the four sides until they are at the same level.

JEWELRY EXERCISES 75

Cut four prongs—the triangular figures in the corners—so that when soldered they are 3 mm or 4 mm taller than the upper edge of the box. Solder the prongs and cut off the base of the setting, thus eliminating the rectangle which served as the beginning of the layout. File off the lower part, keeping the stone from reaching the base of the setting. Leave enough for the curve you should make in this lower part to coincide with the curve of the shank (d). File the lateral angles of the prongs so they are no longer angular, but straight.

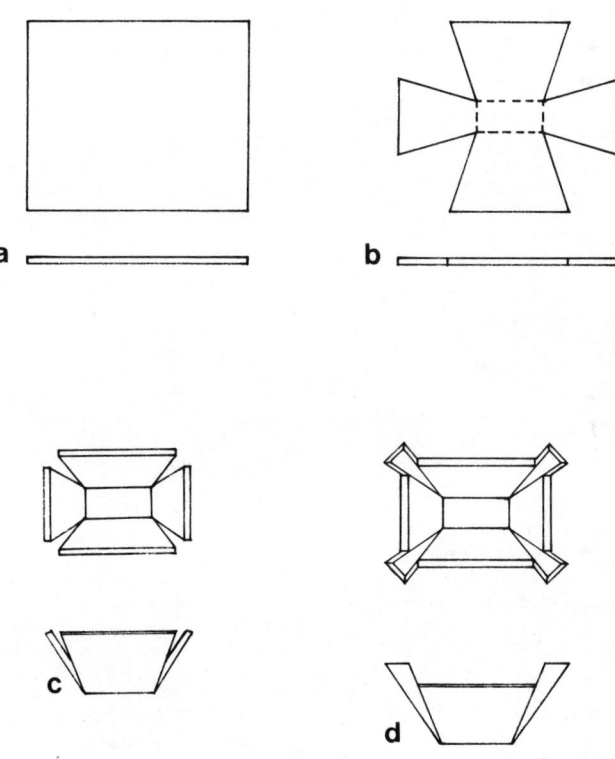

Make the shank so that the upper part, where the solder is, is wider than the lower part (e). Cut in the center and make the cuts shown in (f). You will have removed part of the center of the ring and two points will be left on each side, which will be bent toward the outside. These points will support the lower part of the setting.

Before soldering the setting on the ring you must make a curve on its lower part, on the inside of the shank, as done in previous exercises. This curve is the equivalent of the curve of the ring size.

The soldering process is the same as that described in previous exercises. Tack one of the points on the setting. If the position is correct, solder the four points, beginning with the side opposite the one tacked. The last operation is to cut the small pieces of metal which go from the central cut of each side on the shank to halfway up the sides of the setting. The detail of this is shown in (g).

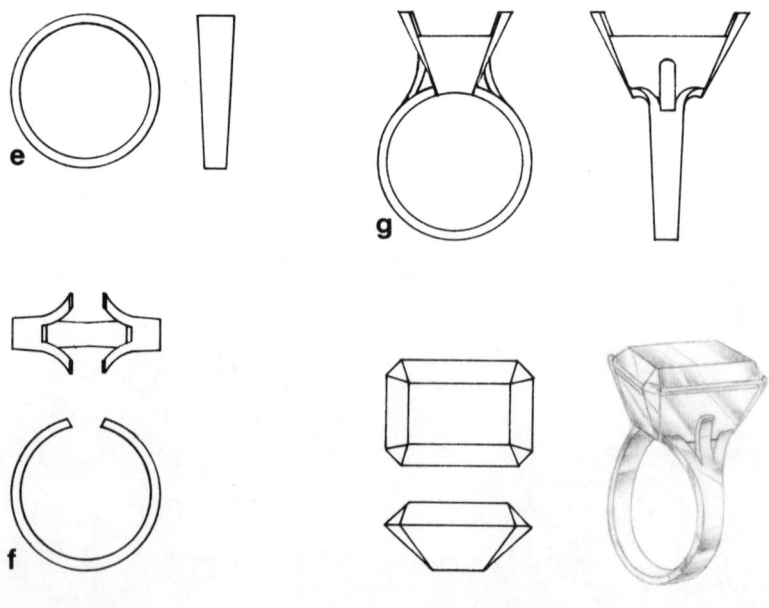

EXERCISES 43 AND 44

Objective: Eternity bands with stones

These two exercises present a type of ring with stones distributed at equal distances around the entire perimeter. The stones used, as well as the construction technique, are totally different from each other: one uses baguette-cut stones, and the other round ones. The first is made from sheet and the other is carved into the shank.

EXERCISE 43: Eternity Ring with Baguette Stones and Bed or Channel Setting

Metal: Silver; rings, both sides, in metal 1 mm thick; inside supports in rectangular wire, 1 mm × 2 mm
Stones: Baguette cut, 12 to 14, 1.5 mm to 2 mm wide, 4.5 mm long
Scale: 1:1 (Detail in (d) is enlarged)

Cut two rings as indicated in (a). The inside diameter is the finger measurement. It is usually wise to leave a little margin and make the inside diameter slightly smaller, to be able to file it after soldering and cutting the excess of the divisions between the stones. The outside diameter is slightly greater than the sum of the length of all the stones, since these must go between the two walls and slightly under the line of the edges.

Both the opening between the walls of the ring and the number of interior divisions will depend on the size of the stones. The stones will touch each other and will be supported only by their sides between the edge of the walls of the ring.

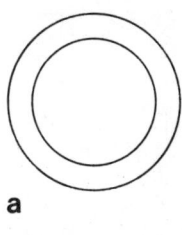

a

Once the rings are made, proceed to distribute the stones and to place the supports of all the interior divisions. In the case of this ring, first place four supports or interior divisions. The placement of these determines the height of the stones. The setter's job is to lower the angles of these supports so that the stone is properly seated. Solder these four on one side of the ring, having first drawn a line with the compass which defines the height of the supports (b). Also mark all the points where the other supports should go. Now you can solder the other side of the ring (c) and continue to solder the supports one by one. This is fairly easy if, when cutting the supports, you adjust them quite well so that they remain in place without moving. You can also solder all the supports on one side of the ring and put on the other side at the end.

Once the two sides of ring are soldered, proceed to cut all the tips of the supports which will project toward the inside of the ring; (d) shows how they will fit inside once cut. Then file and sand the inside, leaving the required measurement.

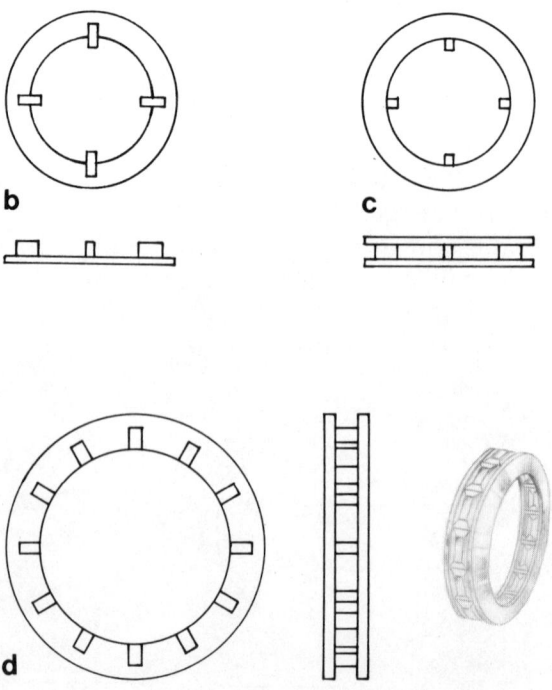

EXERCISE 44: Eternity Ring with Round Stones in Prong Settings

Metal: Sterling silver, bar 3 mm thick and 5.5 mm wide
Stones: Arrangement of 16, φ 3 mm
Scale: 1:1

Make a ring with a section 5 mm wide and 3 mm thick. In this exercise, the size of the ring allows for 16 stones of 3 mm diameter.

Once the ring is made, file it laterally so that it is 5 mm on the inside and 4 mm on the outside from its axis (a). Then distribute the stones, marking the respective points with small crosses. In each point marked make a small perforation, 1 mm or 1.5 mm diameter, which can be moved with a bur if not correctly centered. Then, with a conical bur, open the perforations until they are the diameter of the stones. The opening of the lights will be done after the divisions of the settings are marked, using the same conical bur so that it will have the same diameter as the stones. Mark the sides of the settings, or the distribution of these among the stones (b).

With a saw, make the cuts which define the settings, making the cut cross from one side of the ring to the other. All the lines of the cuts should be projected from the center, or axis, of the ring toward the outside edge (c, center). With a rat-tail needle file, make a channel the whole length of the perimeter of the ring; this channel is seen in (c, upper). It should be the same depth as the exterior cuts in each setting, made with the same file (c, center). With these cuts you will have made the prongs for all the settings.

Throughout this exercise you must be very precise in your cuts.

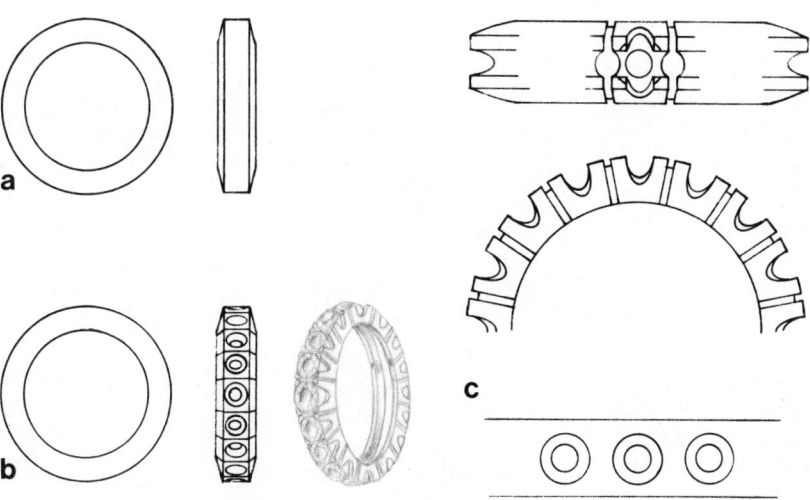

EXERCISE 45: Man's Ring with Diamonds

Metal: Silver; plate for shank in metal 1.3 mm thick; side arches 1.5 mm thick; upper sheet for stones, 1.2 mm thick
Stones: Arrangement of 25, ɸ 2 mm to ɸ 2.5 mm; pavé setting
Scale: 1:1

Cut a piece of metal as indicated in (a), and bend it, being careful not to deform it, as seen in (b). On the ends of both sides make half circles, leaving a small step on each side of the length of the line of the axis (b). Cut two lateral arches as shown in (c); the inside curve of these arches should correspond exactly to a segment of the interior circumference of the ring. These two arches are soldered so that the upper line coincides with the small steps on the sides of the ring. Cut the upper piece where the stones will go, and bend it so that it fits on the upper curve and is lightly supported on the lateral arches (d). Before soldering this part of the ring, distribute the stones on it as in previous exercises. Open lights, too; this can be done with a saw or with the conical bur. The finished ring seen from three sides is shown in (e).

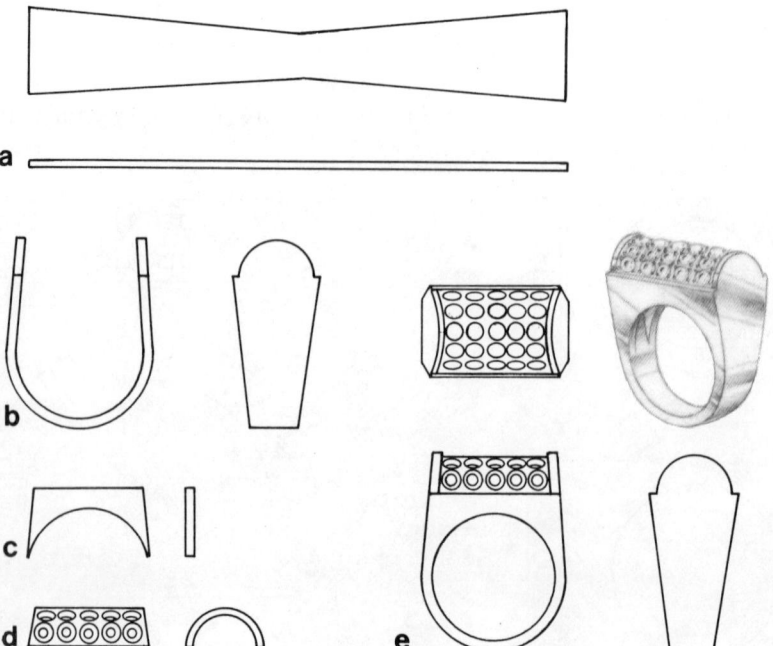

EXERCISE 46: Basket Ring

Metal: Silver; upper sheet for settings, 1.4 mm thick; wires for basket, φ 0.8 mm; section of oval basket, 1 mm × 1.2 mm
Stones: φ 3.5 mm for outside; center stone, 6 mm × 10 mm; distance between stones and edges, 0.5 mm
Scale: 1:1

Beginning with a rectangle (a), draw an ellipse and give it the convex form seen in (b, lower). Distribute the stones. The size of the ellipse depends on the size of the stones.

On a surface like this, where stones of the same type are placed around a central one, place the center one first. To mount an oval stone on the plaque, proceed exactly as with round stones: prepare a seat with angled walls. For the round stones, use a conical bur. For the stone in this exercise, use a saw, as in making the inside lights in the first exercises dealing with stones. Once the seat of the central stone is made, make those for the round stones. Remember to leave a distance of 0.5 mm between the stones and the edges. Only when the seats of the stones are done should you give the piece its exterior form, using a needle file (c). Between the central stone and the outer ones are small perforations. In these perforations, solder wires 0.8 mm in diameter, which will be prongs for both the inside and outside stones.

With the upper part ready, begin to make the basket, or lower structure, made of wires. First, make an oval frame (d). Around this oval solder the wires, which will be exterior prongs of the stones.

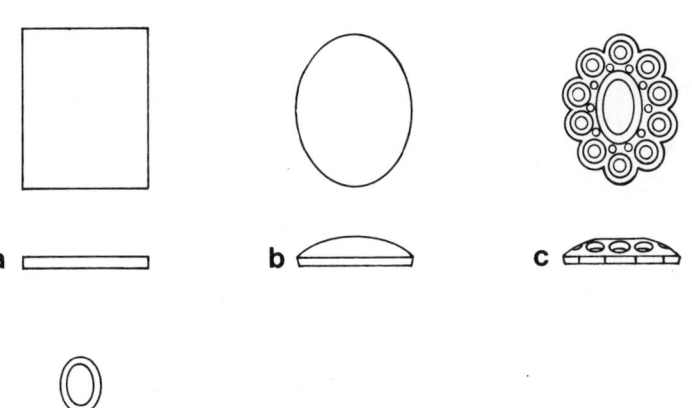

82 THE JEWELER'S CRAFT

Once the wires are soldered (e), one for each stone on the outside of the half-circle and one for each meeting point between the half-circles, proceed to make the basket. This is done so that the projecting part of the center ellipse (e, lower) is on the outer part of the basket (f). On this projecting part you will later file the curve of the inside of the ring. So as not to damage the excess of the oval, first emboss a piece of sheet, in the center of which an oval will be opened, slightly larger than the center of the basket. On this embossed sheet, which is left inside the dapping block, carefully emboss the ring with the wires, making the central oval coincide with the opening in the sheet. Do not hit hard on the wires as you might damage them.

With the basket ready, solder the upper plaque of the stones. The height is shown in (g), a simplified drawing. It also shows the position of the prongs.

When the basket is finished, make the shank. The technique is the same as in Exercise 40, forging the shank ring and then cutting it to make it fit the basket (h).

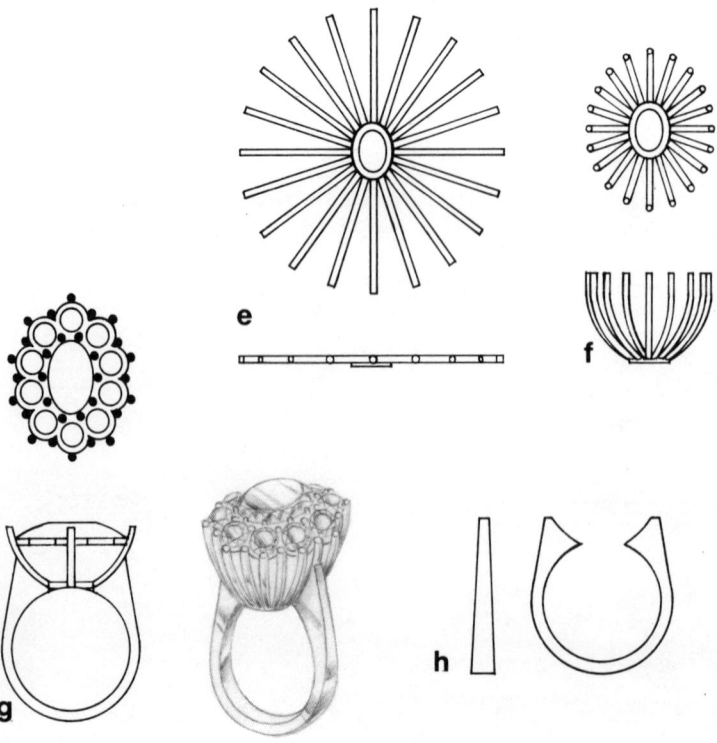

JEWELRY EXERCISES

EXERCISE 47: Cuff Links

Metal: Sterling silver; upper sheet for setting, 1.5 mm thick; section of lower frame, wire 0.5 mm × 1.5 mm; support for findings, 0.5 mm thick; finding, square tube 3.5 mm per side, in metal 0.4 mm thick; half-round wire for fork, 1.1 mm × 2.2 mm; square rivet, 1.4 mm per side; watch spring
Stones: 16 stones, ⌀ 2 mm; center stone, 7 mm per side, cabochon cut
Scale: 1:1

The steps illustrated in (a) and (b) have been previously described. Once you have completed (b), make the cut for the central cabochon stone. Remember that you are making a pair of pieces, and that all the steps are repeated immediately for the second piece.

Lower the metal around the center stone, leaving 0.5 mm of metal as a border, 0.5 mm deep. The result is shown in (c). The distribution of the stones around the central stone is shown in (d); the rear part should have the lights, three of which are shown (d, lower).

Make a frame as shown in (e), which will correspond exactly to the form of the piece just made. Solder this to the rear part of the top, having first lowered the top's edges with a file so that the frame is seated properly. Solder the frame.

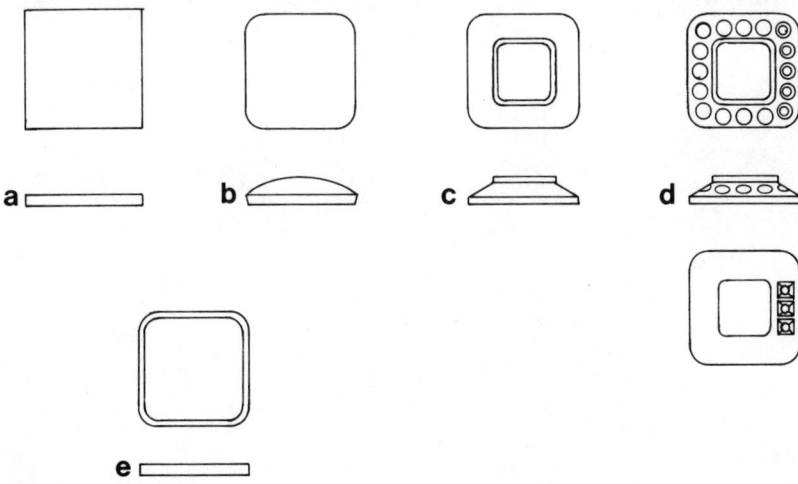

The bridge (f) is soldered on the rear part as a base for the center stone of each cuff link, and also as a support for the link system. Once these two parts are made, solder the center of the rear part as shown in (g); the lights have been omitted only for simplification. This bridge should be soldered so that it does not cover the lights.

Begin constructing the link system (h). The first step is to make a square-section tube; the measurements of the tube are given in the technical information at the beginning of the exercise. If the tube is 3.5 mm per side, the total width of the metal needed is 3.5 × 4, or 14 mm.

The metal is 0.4 mm thick. Cut a piece of it 14 mm wide and about 8 cms (80 mm) long. As described in Exercise 31 (locket), close this metal to form a round tube, using a design block as a base and an interior wire to allow you to close the tube; in the final step, use a hammer. Draw the tube through a square-hole drawplate, preferably using a square section piece inside the tube so that the sides do not collapse, and begin to give shape to the square-section tube. Follow the steps exactly as described in Exercise 31. Before soldering the tube, take out the inside piece. Solder and continue to draw it through the drawplate until you have the required section.

Cut the two pieces you need for the cuff links, make a perforation on one side and at the center that goes through to the other side (h). With a piece of square wire of the same measurement as the outside of the tube, make the two end pieces which will close the tube (i). Make two springs from a piece of watch spring for each system, as shown in (j).

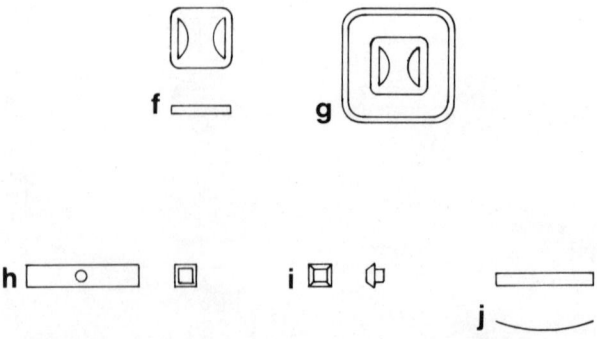

Using half-round wire, make the two forks as shown in (k). Cut two pieces of square wire 1.5 mm per side to use as pins holding the fork and the square tube. This square wire will pass through the perforation in the tube to turn without difficulty.

Assemble the parts. First solder the forks to the bridge of each rear part of the cuff link (l, dotted lines). Solder the end pieces (i) onto one end of the tubes. Then pass the wire through the perforation in the tube and solder the forks onto its ends. Insert the two pieces of watch spring as shown in (l), leaving the square wire between them. You cannot solder again since heating would cause the metal to lose its temper, so you will have to put the other end piece on either by riveting or with soft (lead) solder.

The finished cuff link is seen in (m).

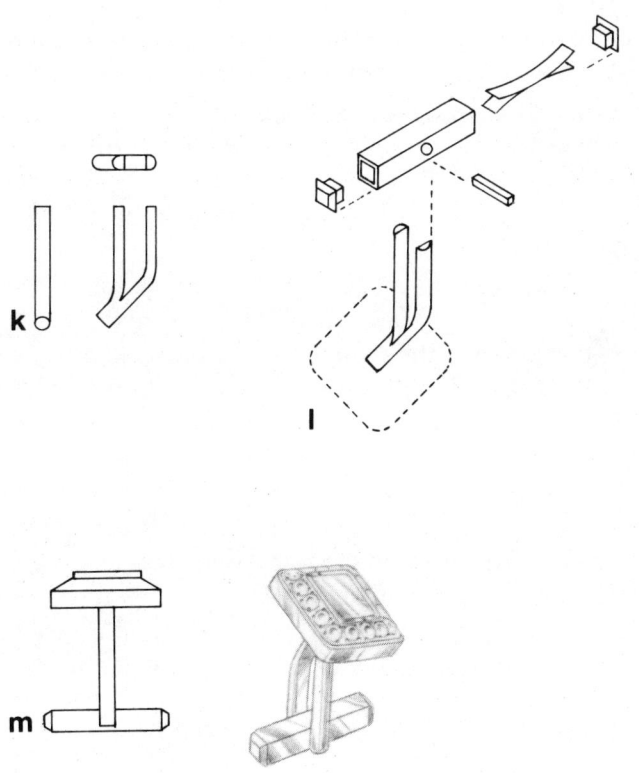

EXERCISE 48: **Illusion Ring**

Metal: Silver; cone and top sheet, 1.5 mm thick; final dimensions of cone, φ 16 mm upper part, φ 12 mm lower part; opening for center setting, φ 6 mm; setting in proportion to center opening; shank, metal 3.5 mm per side
Stones: Center stone, φ 5.5 mm; outside stones, φ 4 mm
Scale: 2:1 for steps and details; 1:1 for final piece

By this point, you should be able to make many pieces simply by observing certain details of the construction and following the technical specifications. Here, I have not drawn more steps for each figure in the exercise than those strictly necessary. Since the scale is 2:1, divide the measurements taken from the drawings in half.

Three parts are shown in (a): the cone (center) on which the setting will be constructed; the base (lower), to be soldered onto the cone once the cuts have been made in the upper and lower parts of the cone and the top disc has been cut and soldered to the cone; and the top disc (upper), which will hold all the stones and the central setting. Make these three parts so that they match up. The top disc should be inside the cone and have the same inside angle as the cone.

In (b) we see the seats made in the top for the outside stones and for the central setting. Make these seats before the top is soldered onto the cone. Once they are made, solder the top.

The parts of (a) fit directly onto each other when the cuts are made (c). On the lower part of the cone, make the triangular cuts shown in (c). The distribution of these cuts will place one beneath each stone and one between each stone. Now make the cuts of the upper part, leaving an independent prong in front of each stone. Analyzing (c) and (d), you will understand the form of the cuts and the shape they will have. Now solder the base of the cone, as in (c).

To make the shank, follow the steps detailed in previous exercises. The base of the cone should have an arch corresponding to the arch of the inside of the shank.

The finished piece is sketched in (e).

JEWELRY EXERCISES 87

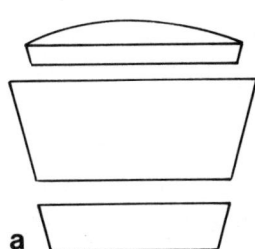

a

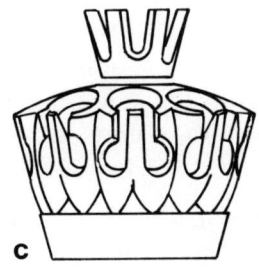

c

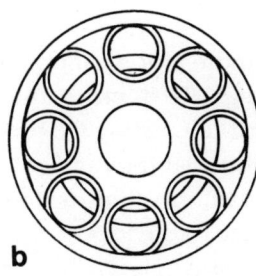

b

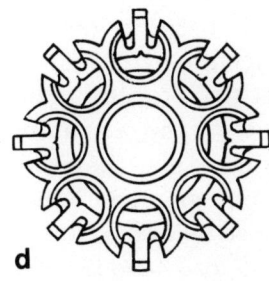

d

e

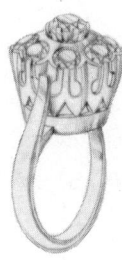

88 THE JEWELER'S CRAFT

EXERCISE 49: **Clasp for String Bracelet or Necklace**

Metal: Silver; upper sheet for settings, 1 mm thick; clip (presser tongue), φ 0.6 mm thick; keyway, φ 0.4 mm thick; tube settings, φ 0.6 mm thick; lower base, φ 0.6 mm thick; gallery, φ 0.5 mm thick
Stones: Center stone, φ 3 mm; all other stones, φ 2 mm
Scale: 1:1 for steps and final piece; 2:1 for tube settings

Cut two pieces as shown in (a), taking the measurements from the size of stones used, and emboss them to a curve not greater than that in (b).

With these two pieces embossed, cut down the segments of the arc where the other piece overlaps and adjust the angles when they are linked, as in (c). Interlace them and solder them at the meeting points. You may have to make some changes in the curvature of the parts in order to interlace them correctly.

Once the parts are adjusted, distribute the stones and make the lights (c). Proceed with the tube settings. First make the tube, measuring the diameter of the stones and calculating 0.5 mm extra per side to give the setting effect. With this diameter, calculate the width of the metal. The process is the same as that described in Exercise 31 for the construction of the hinge of the locket. Once the tube is ready and its seam soldered, mark the height of the prongs with a compass and make the cuts of the prongs. Make these one at a time. File and sand, and then cut the necessary length of the setting. The tube and its cuts, to scale 2:1 are shown in (d).

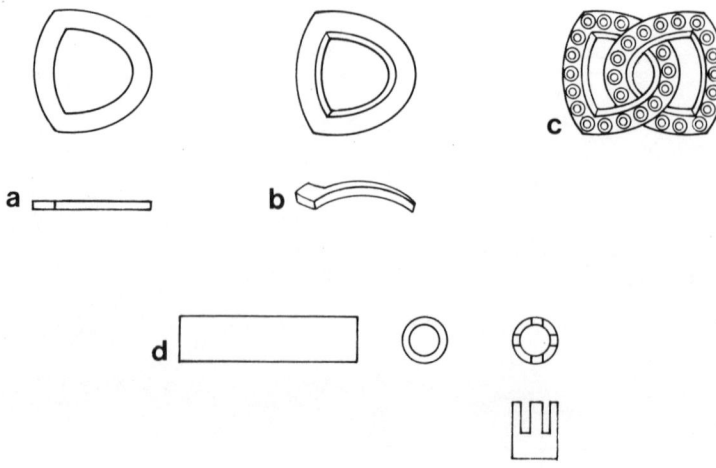

Now make the keyway and the presser tongue (e) as described in Exercise 32 (h). First cut the sheet for the presser tongue as in (f). Make the keyway according to the width of this sheet. The construction of the keyway was described in Exercise 32, the simple bracelet. Make two small perforations shown in (f, upper), and from these holes make a cut parallel to the sides and long enough for the resulting tongue to have an adequate spring when raised to position. Solder the presser on the tongue and solder a bar on the rear part of its base. The bar will serve as a butt when introduced in the keyway, the jump rings are soldered to it, and the strings will be tied to it.

Before soldering the keyway to the back of the overlapped (interlaced) pieces, solder the tube settings; their positions are shown in (g). With a bur or round file, make enough cuts in the metal to allow sufficient surface contact for the tube settings so they don't move in later soldering operations.

Place the finished piece (c), on a plasticine or wax base, and inside it, supported on the plasticine, place the tube settings. Once these are in position, cover the whole piece with plaster of Paris or casting investment. This will hold all the pieces in place during the soldering. When the plaster hardens, take off the plasticine. Make sure all the plasticine is removed, as residues will disturb the soldering. Apply flux and solder to the settings and heat the whole piece evenly until the solder runs and holds the settings.

When the settings are soldered, solder the keyway. The practice in Exercise 32 will have given a good understanding of the system. Keep in mind that the tongue of the clip must prevent the clip from leaving its position if it is not released by the presser bar. This requires a proper support on the inside of the structure.

90 THE JEWELER'S CRAFT

With the system working, make the gallery and solder the base, or rear cover. The gallery is a strip of metal which follows the entire perimeter of the figure, and which has been pierced to allow light to enter from the side of the piece. Cut a piece of metal and shape it according to the outside form of the piece, making the various heights fit all around the perimeter. Once this form is done, make the cuts in it you consider necessary. Solder it onto the upper piece. In (g) you can see part of the gallery, not entirely drawn so as to show the interior system behind it.

Finally, solder the base of the gallery, which should also be pierced to allow greater entrance of light. This base will have the same form as the outside of the piece and the edge of the gallery.

On the opposite side of the clasp, solder small jump rings, which are the same as those soldered on the rear bar of the clip.

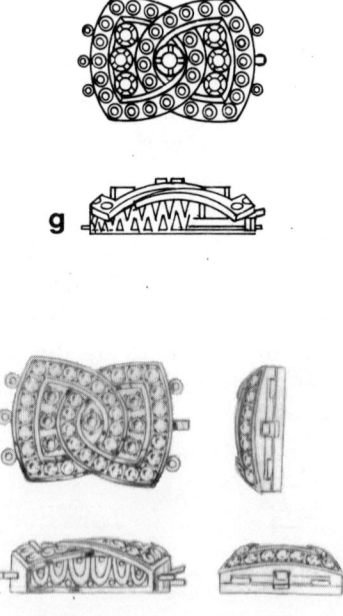

EXERCISES 50 AND 51

Objective: Linked tube settings
Metal: Sterling silver

In these exercises only a few specifications will be given as to metal thickness or setting dimensions. It is advisable to make two bracelets using settings in a single line in the first system and a double row of settings in the second. It is important for the bracelets to have enough articulation to bend easily around the wrist, and for the distances between the settings to be equal.

Use any of the clasps previously described. The prongs should be crossed in an X when seen from above.

The specifications for the bracelets are as follows:

First system: notch 0.7 mm wide (approx.) and 0.8 mm to 1 mm from bottom; wire for links, ϕ 0.5 mm or 0.6 mm
Second system: drill hole ϕ 0.6 mm; distance between drill hole and notch, 0.8 mm; wire for links, ϕ 0.6 mm

EXERCISE 50: Linking with Jump Rings

In the first system the rings are soldered to the setting on the side opposite the loop (c), and the excess metal is filed from the inside.

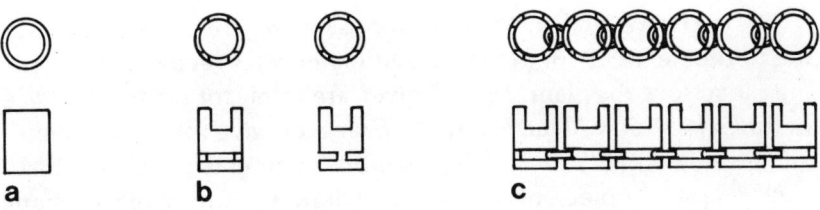

EXERCISE 51: Linking with Hooks

In the second system there is a perforation and a notch under it on one side of the setting and on the other side there is just one perforation, which should be exactly the same in diameter as the wire hook. The hook is soldered on the second perforation (b). It then enters the perforation of the next setting (a), bends inside and comes out by way of the notch. Close the bend of the hook so that it butts against the wall of the first setting and solder it there (c, section).

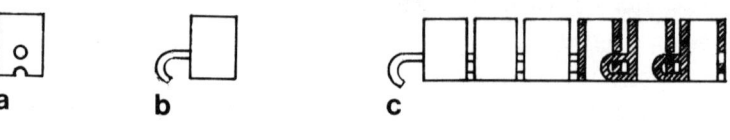

a   b   c

EXERCISE 52: Pin, Leaves, and Diamonds

Objective: To represent movement and fluidity in metal
Metal: Silver; two leaves (a), 0.7 mm thick; one leaf (c), 0.5 mm thick; two leaves (d), 0.4 mm thick; tubes for settings, ϕ 3 mm, reduced to ϕ 2.5 mm, ϕ 2 mm, and ϕ 1.5 mm, in metal sheet 0.35 mm thick; wire for settings, from ϕ 0.7 mm, reduced for each setting in proportion to the tubes
Stones: ϕ 3 mm to ϕ 1.5 mm
Scale: Leaves, 1:1; setting of ϕ 3 mm, 2:1

This is a free exercise. The indications given here may vary according to the necessity or availability of materials. I recommend copying a leaf from any plant. Figures given are solely for relating the size of the parts. You will have to form the leaves, give them movement, and group them in a logical, harmonious manner while giving life to each one. On a piece of paper, try to draw a group of leaves many times until this relationship is understood and comes easily.

For the mechanics of the exercise, use various pliers and any tool which will allow you to make metal sheets into leaves. The veins can be engraved with an engraver, and texture given to the surface with a texture bur or other texture tool. The leaves are all to be mounted on a single branch, to which you will have to give texture as well as form.

The settings are done with tube and wire. Prepare the tubes to the measurements given. Cut them a little longer than the length of two settings in line. The wires, which will be the prongs, are soldered on the outside of the tubes. Cut and bend as shown in (e), and solder as in (f). The opening between the sides of the wire will depend on the diameter of the tube. Once the two U shapes are soldered to the tube (f), cut in the middle and also on the two ends of the wires to make two settings like the one shown in (g).

Solder the settings following a decreasing line from the center of the leaf toward both ends, or from the upper part of the leaf toward the tip.

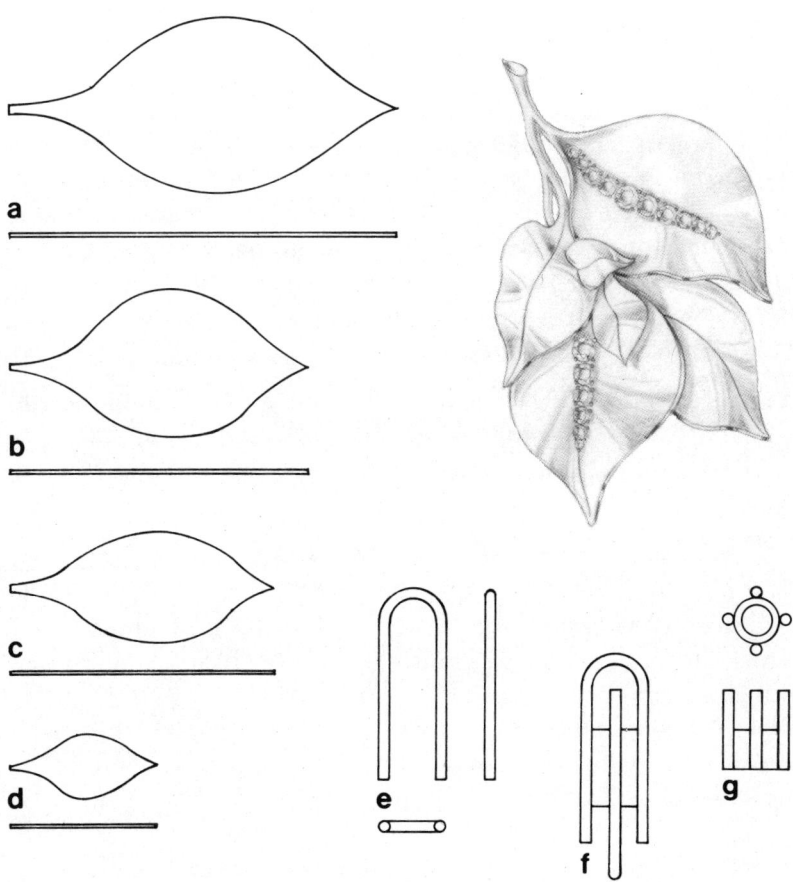

USEFUL FINDINGS EXERCISES

Findings are usually bought ready-made, since the time spent making them by hand is not usually appreciated in the final piece. These exercises are included because they have not been described in the preceding exercises, and it is occasionally necessary to make a finding by hand.

EXERCISE 53: **Pin Stem and Catch**

Metal: Same as the piece for which the system is being made; joint, ϕ 0.5 mm thick; wire for pin stem, ϕ 1.1 mm; pin-stem holder, ϕ 0.6 mm thick; bayonet catch, outside tube, ϕ 2 mm in metal 0.3 mm thick; inside tube, ϕ 1.5 mm in metal 0.3 mm thick Scale: 2:1

The pin stem is used for any type of pin. It can be used in the exercises involving pins and stones (Exercises 37, 38, and 52).

The joint part is made by cutting a sheet as in (a), and bending it as in (b). The insided space should have the same width as the piece of metal soldered on the pin stem. Form it as shown in (c). This part is *not* soldered to the piece, as might be thought from (c, center). The lower view shows a cut which supports the pin stem and which also serves as a spring. The piece is soldered with two parts touching: the circular part and the point of the side opposite to the opening of the pin-stem support.

USEFUL FINDINGS EXERCISES 95

To make the catch, make two tubes, according to the specifications given, so one fits tightly inside the other (d) and (e). Then solder a base, or support, on the outside tube (f). On this tube, make a lengthwise cut, as shown in (f), which will be a slot for a small wire soldered on the inside tube to act as a stop. On the inside tube, make a small cut where the pin will enter when the piece is moved toward the back. Insert the second tube in the larger one with its cut and its slot, and solder a butt or thumbpiece on the rear part (f). The catch is ready to be soldered to the pin.

Solder a piece of metal on the rear of the pin-stem wire; this will be the hinge or turning point of the pin. The finished piece is shown in (g). This piece is riveted to the joint when the piece is finished and polished.

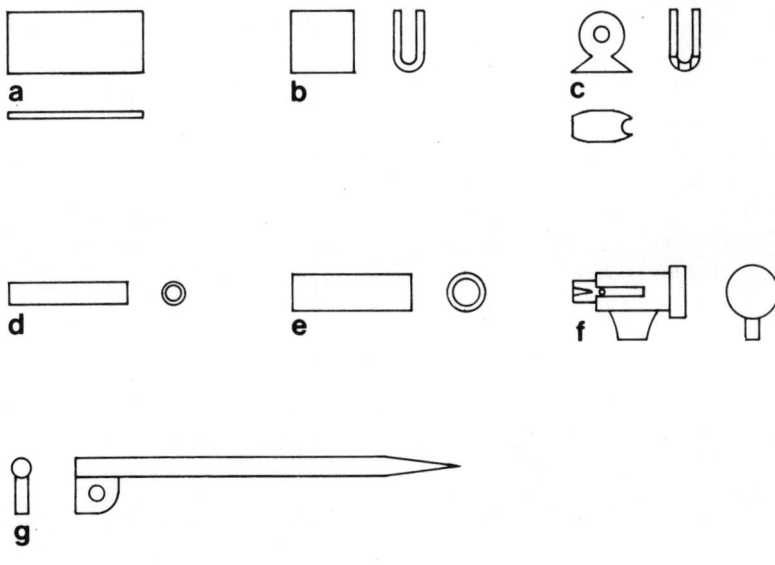

EXERCISE 54: Earring Clip

Metal: Same as the piece for which the system is being made; joint, 4 mm thick; wire for clip, φ 1.4 mm; drill holes, φ 0.7 mm
Scale: 2:1

Beginning with a sheet 4 mm thick, file until achieving a piece as shown in (a). Bend this part as in (b). Cut an insert for the wire. Make perforations for the rivet. The wire is formed as in (c). Once the wire is formed it should *not* be annealed or it will lose its elasticity. The pin is not usually riveted. Bend the tips on both sides, having first made small dents on the line of the lower part of the perforation, so that the wire of the pin fits inside it.

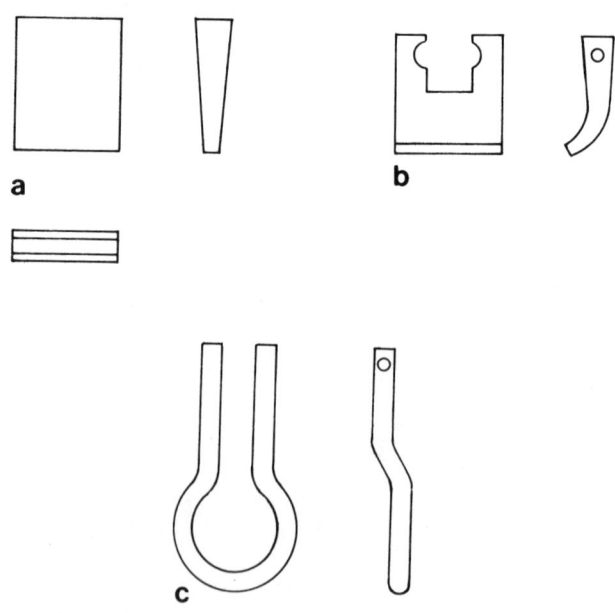

WORKSHOP NOTES

A sketch pad is extremely useful, especially for apprentices but also for experienced jewelers. New techniques, interesting designs, tricks of the trade, repair techniques, and special methods of construction should be jotted down or sketched for future reference. Here I show some examples of specific themes: a page of settings, a page of uses for metal elasticity, a page of rivets, and so on. These pages are not intended to exhaust such themes but to present useful points and an idea of how the jeweler can make his own notes.

The sketches are not precise and are not intended to be. The idea is to get the important point down on paper so as to remember it when needed. It has been said that jewelers never stop learning, and one way to keep learning is to jot down methodically every new concept. Most traditional jewelers are wary of paper and pencil and prefer not to try to draw, but the only way to get over this fear is simply to go ahead and try, slowly gaining the ability to express an idea on paper.

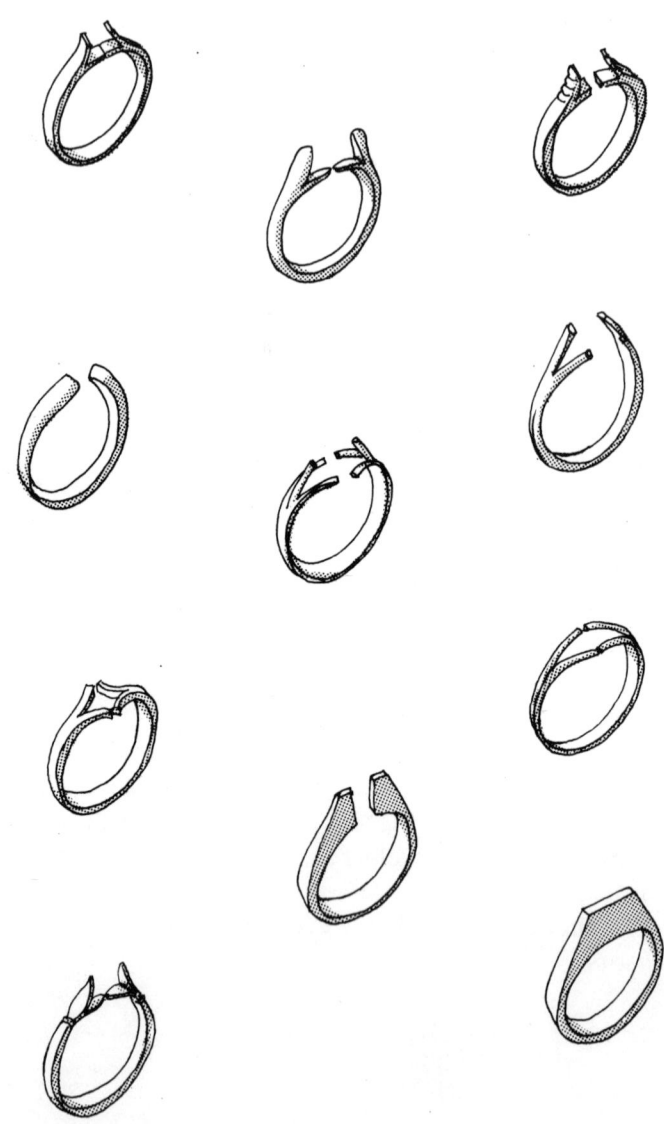

Various shanks

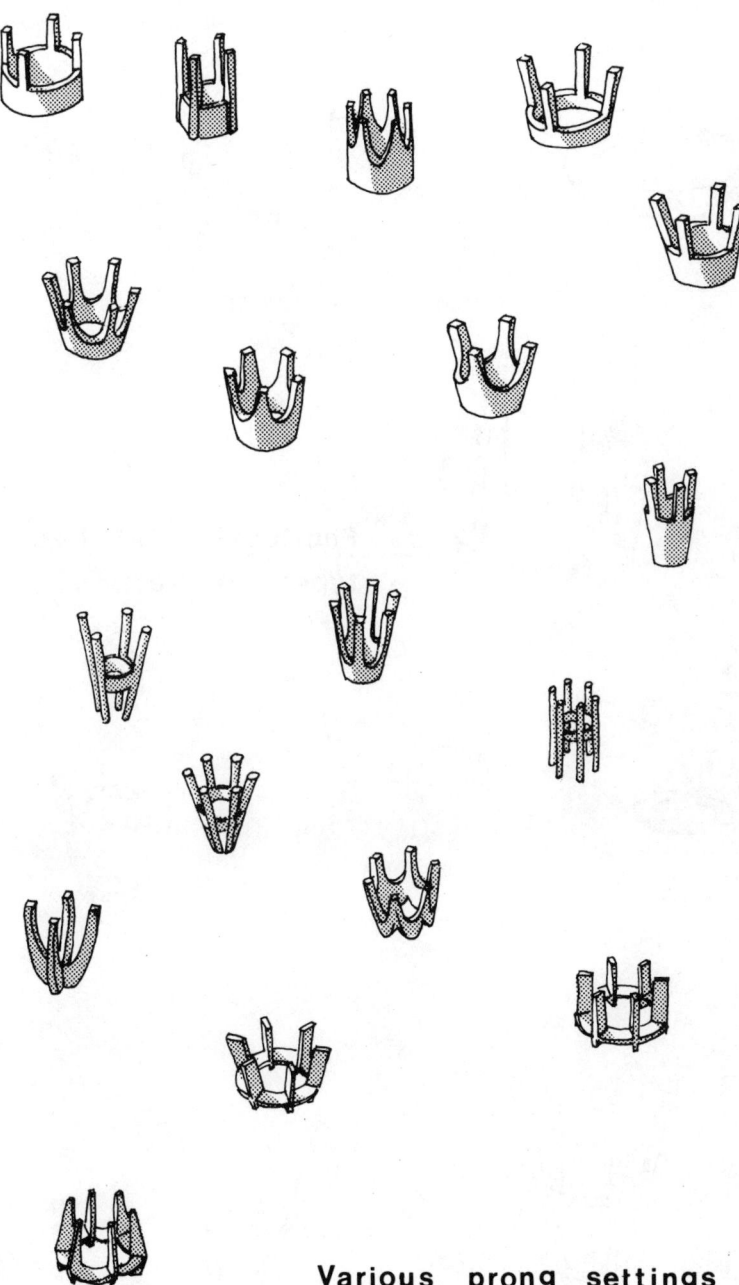

Various prong settings

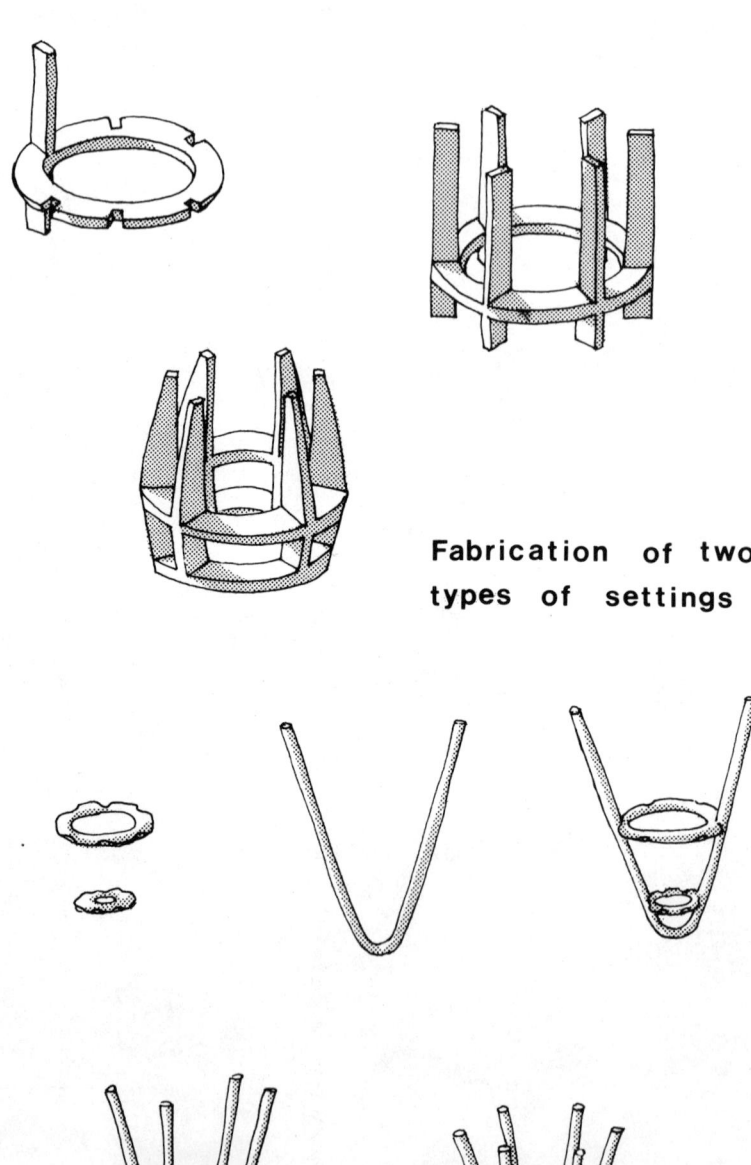

Fabrication of two types of settings

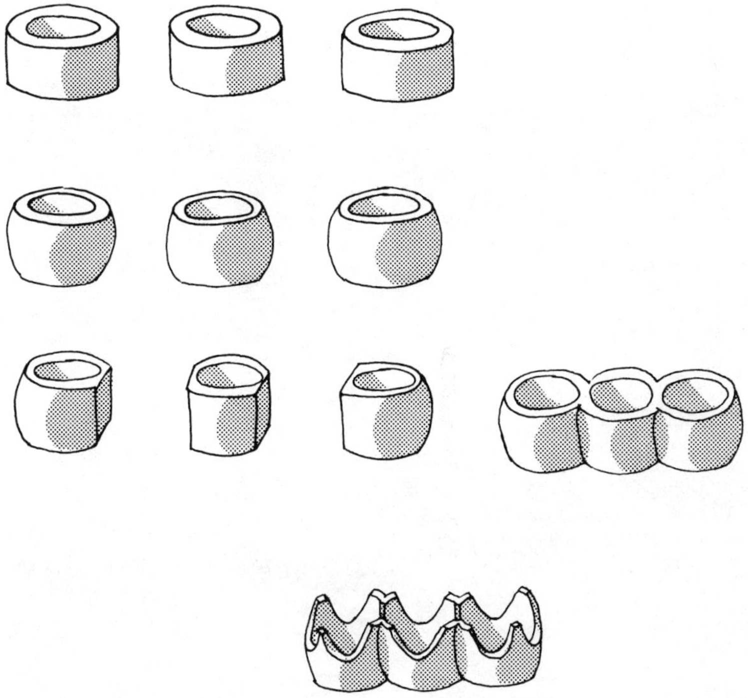

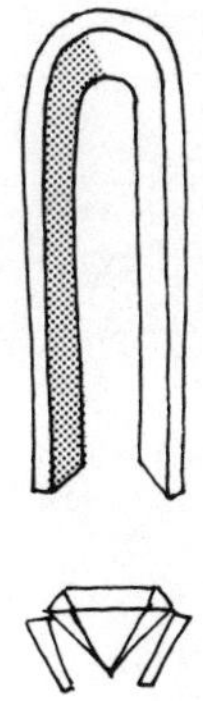

Barrel and box settings

102 THE JEWELER'S CRAFT

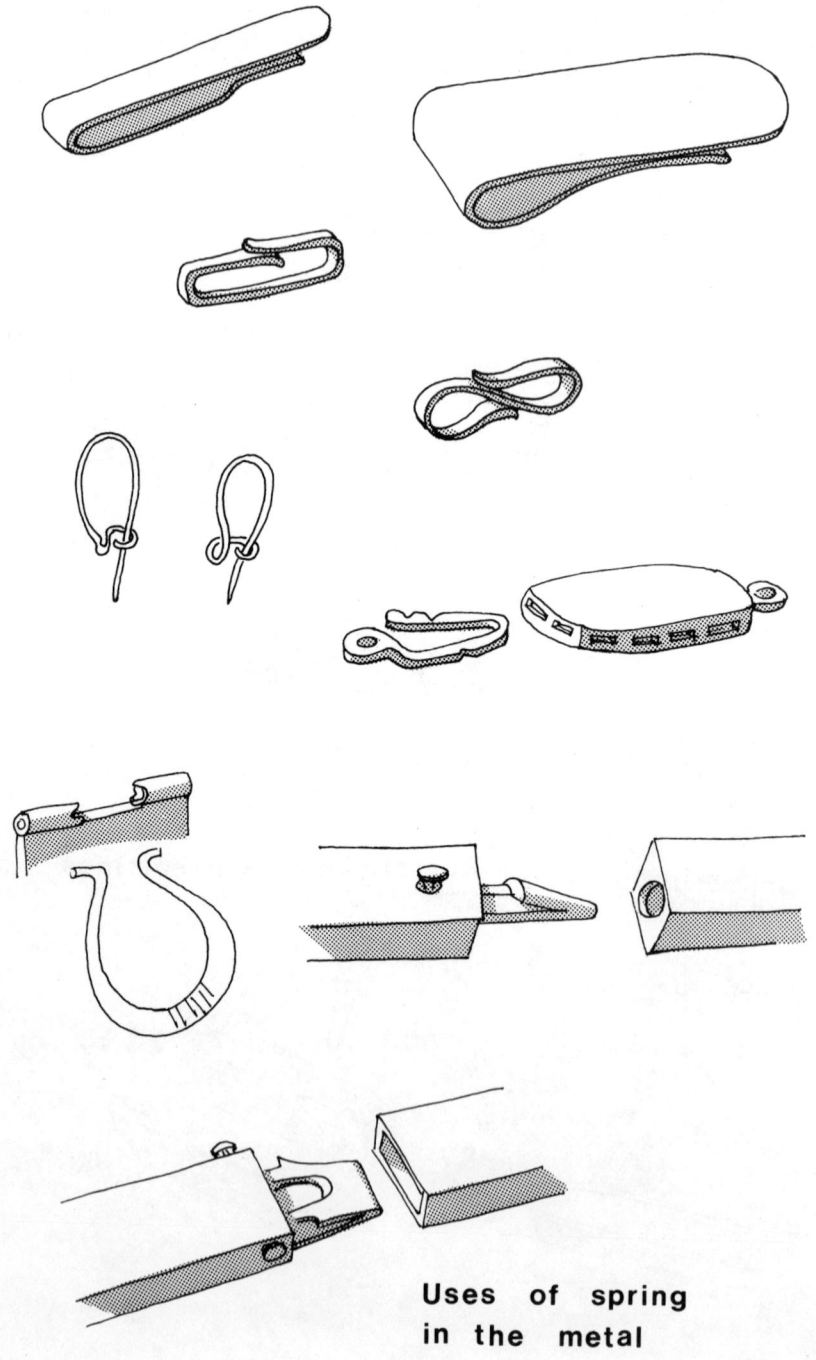

Uses of spring in the metal

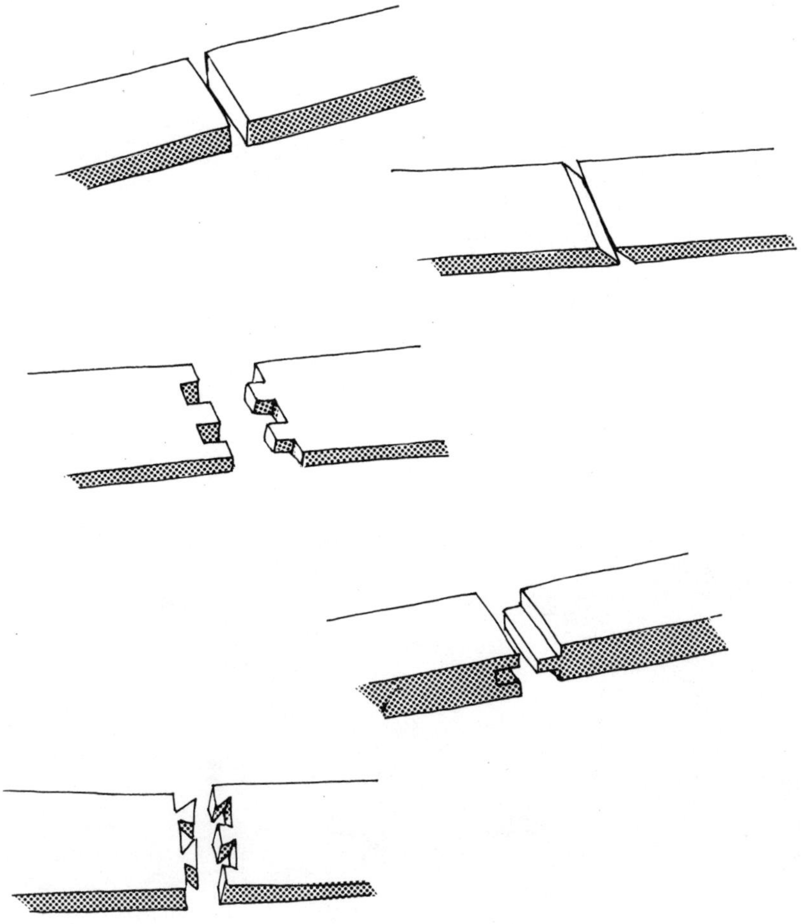

Joints for soldering

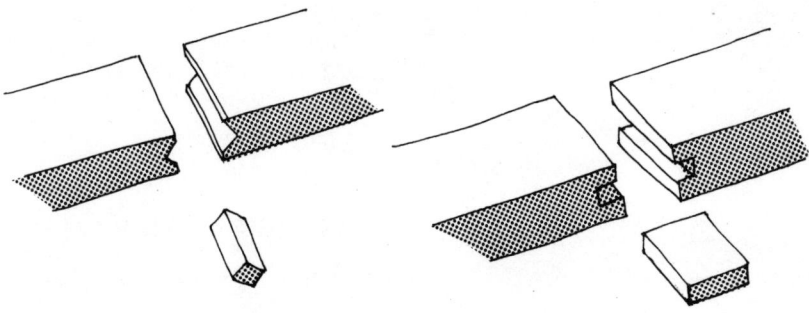

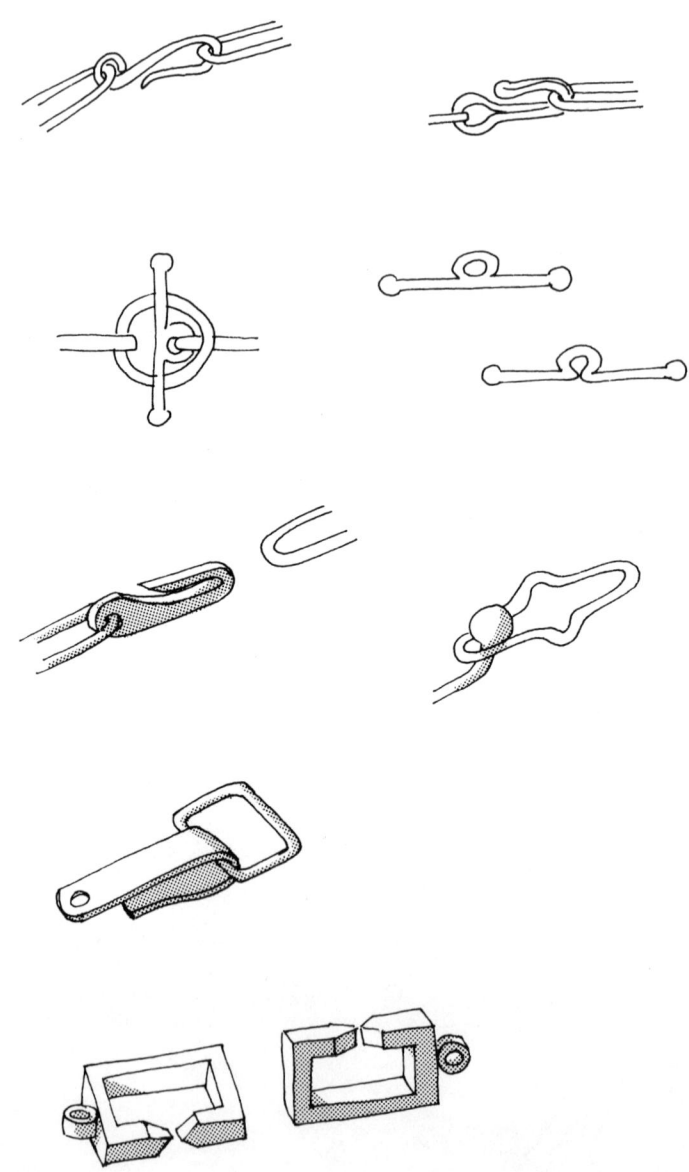

Various catches

WORKSHOP NOTES 105

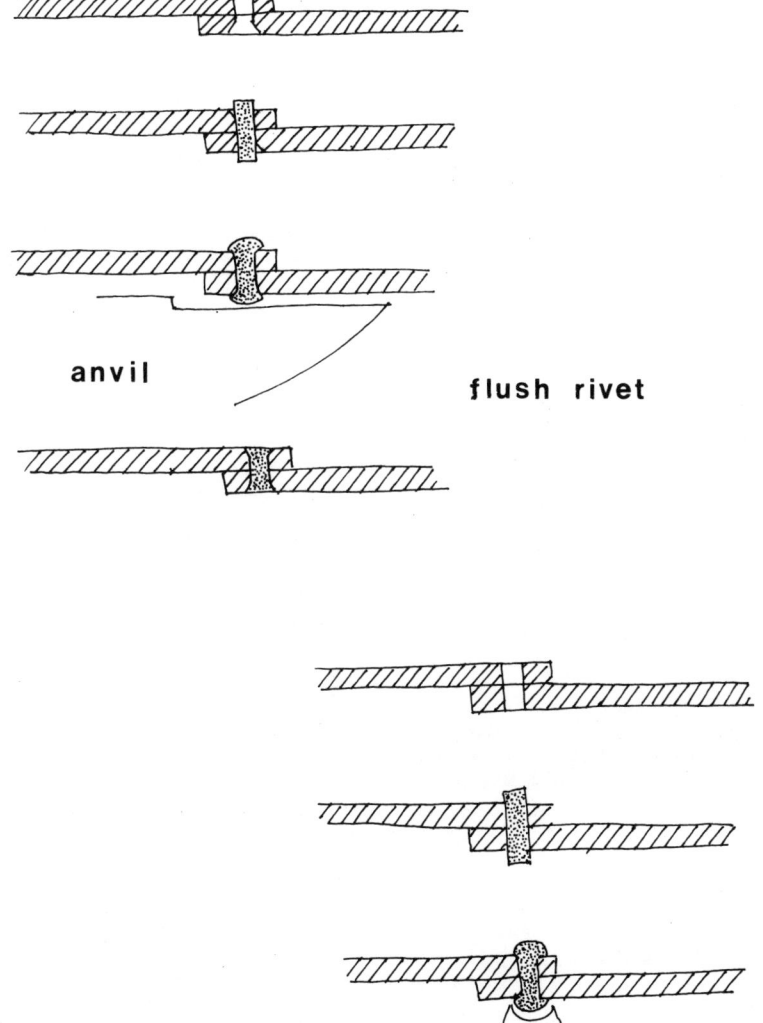

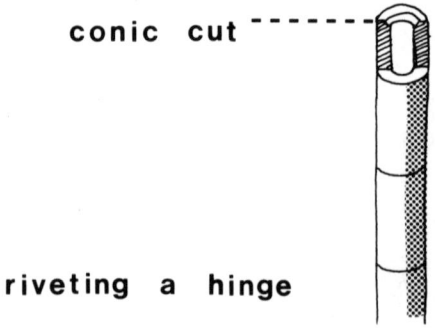

conic cut

riveting a hinge

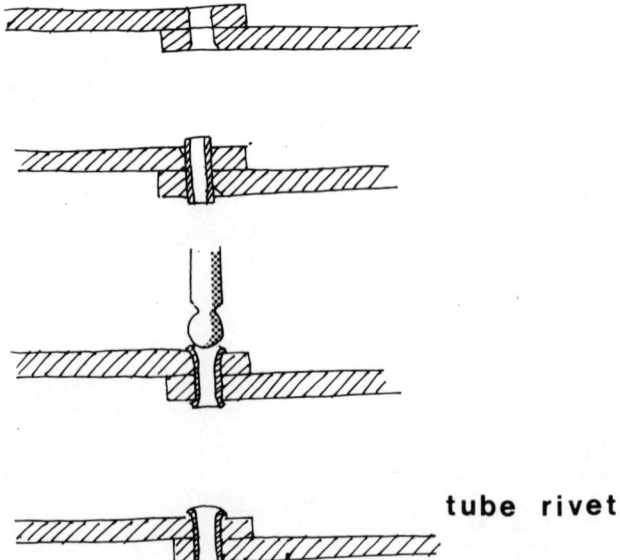

tube rivet

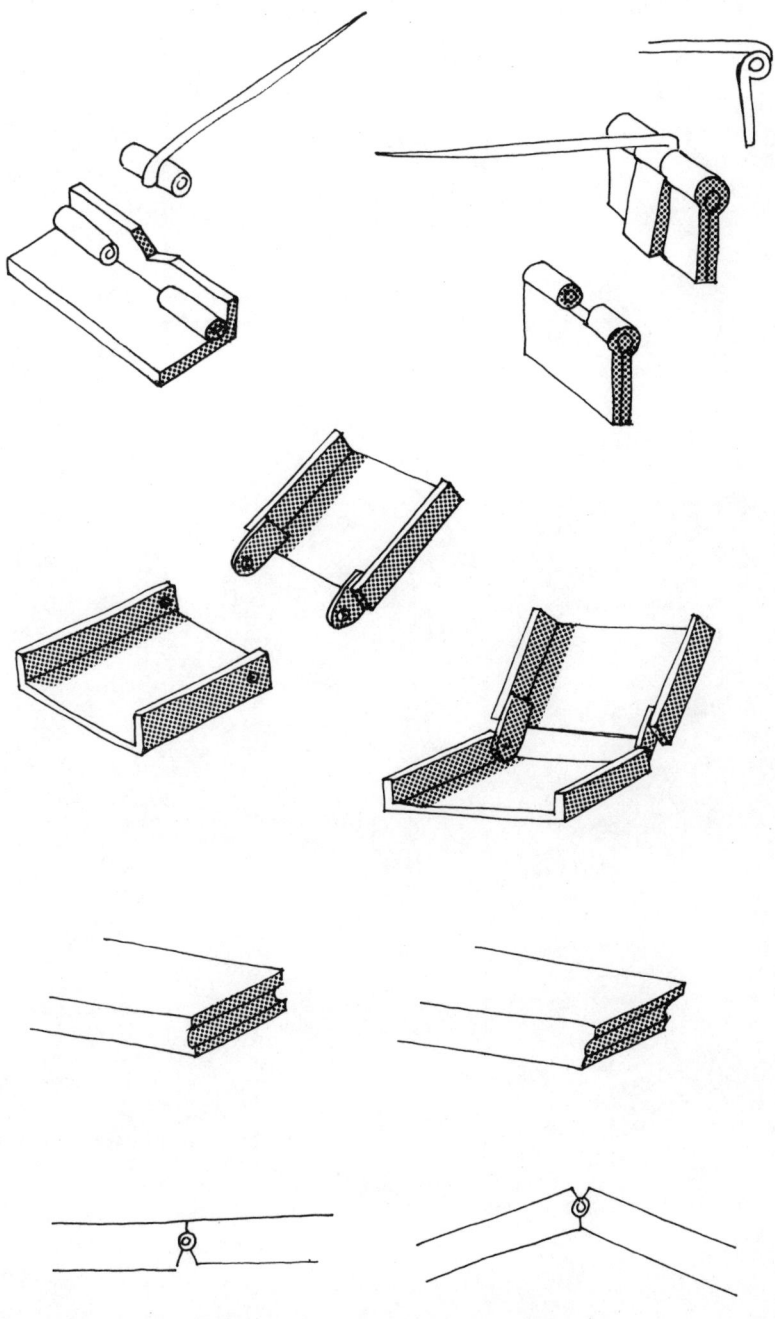

Various uses of hinges

BIBLIOGRAPHY

Bovin, Murray. *Jewelry Making for Schools, Tradesmen, Craftsmen.* New York: Bovin Publishing, 1967.

Braun-Feldweg, Wilhelm. *Metal Design & Technique.* New York: Van Nostrand Reinhold Company, 1975.

Edwards, Ron. *The Technique of Jewelry.* New York: Charles Scribner's Sons, 1977.

Hardy, R. Allen. *The Jewelry Repair Manual,* Second Edition. New York: Van Nostrand Reinhold Company, 1967.

Hardy, R. Allen. *The Jewelry Engravers Manual.* New York: Van Nostrand Reinhold Company, 1967.

McCreight, Tim. *Metalworking for Jewelry.* New York: Van Nostrand Reinhold Company, 1979.

Morton, Philip. *Contemporary Jewelry.* New York: Holt, Rinehart and Winston, 1970.

Smith, Ernest A. *Working in Precious Metals.* London: N.A.G. Press, 1933.

Swest, Inc. *The Technique of Diamond & Stone Setting.* Dallas: Swest, Inc., 1979.

Untracht, Oppi. *Metal Techniques for Craftsmen.* Garden City, N.Y.: Doubleday, 1968.

Von Neumann, Robert. *The Design and Creation of Jewelry.* Philadelphia: Chilton, 1961.

INDEX

angles,
  bisecting, 13
  drawing 45°, 13
  drawing multiple, 13
  drawing right, 12
  sawing between two drilled
    points, 24

basket ring, 81–82
bezels, simple fabrication for
    cabochon and faceted cut
    stones, 39–42
  for cabochon oval stone with
    interior shelf and open
    bottom, 40
  for cabochon round stone with
    closed bottom, 39
  for cabochon round stone with
    interior shelf and open
    bottom, 40
  conical, 41
  square, 42
bibliography, 109
Bovin, Murray, 109
box clasp, 45–46
box-frame setting, ring with, 74–76
bracelets,
  clasp for string, 88–90
  linked tube settings, 91–92
  simple round, 55–58
Braun-Feldwig, Wilhelm, 109

center, establishing in geometric
    figure, 16–17
chain with square wire, 48–50

circles,
  dividing into equal parts, 18
  relation between diameter and
    circumference, 14
  sawing, 23
clasps,
  box, 45–46
  for string bracelet or necklace,
    88–90
conical bezel, 41
Contemporary Jewelry, 109
crown settings. *See also* rings
  with six prongs, 68–70
cube, constructing, 30
cuff links, 43–44
  with stones, 83–84

*Design and Creation of Jewelry,
  The*, 109
diamonds,
  man's ring with, 80
  pins with leaves and, 92–93
drilling, sawing and, 24

earring clip, 96
Edwards, Ron, 109
ellipses, sawing, 23
equilateral triangle, drawing, 14
eternity bands with stones, 65
  baguette stones and bed or
    channel setting, 77–78
  round stones in prong settings,
    79

filing, 34–38

INDEX

findings, 94–96
 earring clip, 96
 pin stem and catch, 94–95
frame, constructing with interior triangles, 30

geometry, basic concepts in, 12–18
goldsmithing exercises, 19–58
 box clasp, 45–46
 chain with square wire, 48–50
 construction of simple forms, soldering, 28–32
 cuff links, 43–44
 filing, 34–38
 locket, portrait holder, 50–55
 piercing, 26–27
 sawing, 20–23
 sawing and drilling, 24
 simple bezel fabrication for cabochon and faceted cut stones, 39–42
 simple round bracelet, 55–58

Hardy, R. Allen, 109
hexagons, drawing, 16
hooks, linking with, 92

illusion ring, 86
inches, compared to millimeters, 10–11

jewelry exercises, 60–96
 basket ring, 81–82
 clasp for string bracelet or necklace, 88–90
 crown setting with six prongs, 68–70
 cufflinks, 83–84
 eternity bands with stones, 65, 77–79
 findings, 94–96
 flat-top or plate setting on curved plane, 63
 flat-top or plate setting on straight plane, 62
 illusion ring, 86
 linked tube settings, 91–92
 man's ring with diamonds, 80

pavé setting on a hemisphere, 63–64
pins, leaves, and diamonds, 92–93
pins with stones, 65–67
ring with box-frame setting, 74–76
rings with four-prong and six-prong crown settings, 71–73
Jewelry Making for Schools, Tradesmen, Craftsmen, 109
Jewelry Repair Manual, The, 109
jump rings, linking with, 91

leaves, pins with diamonds, 92–93
lines, straight,
 bisecting, 12
 dividing into equal parts, 17
linked tube settings, 91–92
 with hooks, 92
 with jump rings, 91
locket, 50–55

McCreight, Tim, 109
man's ring with diamonds, 80
measurements, comparison of, 10–11
Metal Design and Technique, 109
Metal Techniques for Craftsmen, 109
Metalworking for Jewelry, 109
millimeters, compared to inches, 10–11
Morton, Philip, 109

necklace, clasp for string, 88–90

orthographic projection, 8–9

pavé technique. *See* jewelry exercises
pentagons,
 drawing, 16
 sawing, 22
piercing, 26–27
pins,
 leaves and diamonds, 92–93
 stem and catch for, 94–95

with stones, 65–67
portrait holder, 50–55
pyramids,
  constructing square-base, 28
  truncated, for bezel, 42

rhomboids, sawing, 21
right angles, drawing, 12
rings,
  basket, 81–82
  with box-frame setting, 74–76
  channeled, filing, 35
  concave, filing, 36
  double-channeled, filing, 36
  eternity bands with stones, 65
    baguette stones, 77–78
    round stones, 79
  filing bands, 34–38
  with five concentric facets, 37
  flat, filing, 35
  four-prong crown setting and knife-edge shank, 71–72
  half-round, filing, 36
  with harlequin facets, filing, 38
  illusion, 86
  man's, with diamonds, 80
  with six-prong crown setting, 73
  with twelve facets, 37–38
rosettes, layout and piercing of, 26–27

Sawing, 20–23
  angles between two drilled points, 24
  circles, 23
  and drilling, 24
  ellipses, 23
  pentagons, 22
  rhomboids, 21
  squares, 20–21

triangles, 22
scale, in drawing, 10
sectional drawings, 8
sketch pads, 97
Smith, Ernest A., 109
soldering, 28–31
spheres, constructing, 32
square-base pyramid, constructing, 28
square bezel, 42
squares, sawing, 20–21
stones. *See* bezels; jewelry exercises
straight lines,
  bisecting, 12
  dividing into equal parts, 17
string bracelet or necklace, clasp for, 88–90

technical drawing, 8–18
  basic concepts in geometry, 12–18
  comparison of measurements, 10–11
  orthographic projection, 8–9
  scale in, 10
Technique of Jewelry, The, 109
triangles,
  constructing frame with interior, 30
  drawing equilateral, 14
  sawing, 24
truncated pyramid, for bezel, 42

Untract, Oppi, 109

Von Neumann, Robert, 109

Working in Precious Metals, 109
workshop notes, 97